How to Own Your Own Private International Bank

Also by Jerome Schneider

The Complete Guide to Offshore Money Havens

Global Investing for Maximum Profit and Safety

How to Own Your Own Private International Bank

For Profit, Privacy, and Tax Protection

Jerome Schneider

Prima Publishing

Library of Congress Cataloging-in-Publication Data

Schneider, Jerome
   How to own your own private international bank : for profit, privacy, and tax protection / Jerome Schneider.
      p. cm.
   Includes index.
   ISBN 0-7615-1271-3
   1. Private banks—Ownership.   2. Banks and banking, International—Ownership.   I. Title.
HG1978.S36   1998
332.1'5—dc21   98-6088
                                                                    CIP

98 99 00 01 HH 10 9 8 7 6 5 4 3 2 1

Printed in the United States of America

To those who have ever been slighted or underestimated by their bankers. This is the ultimate revenge.

This book is about creating your own private international bank. To get started, the author offers financial advice through workshops and one-on-one private consultation. For more information, Mr. Schneider invites you to contact him through his office in Vancouver at (604) 682-4000 or fax (604) 682-7700.

CONTENTS

ACKNOWLEDGMENTS

This book was written with the encouragement, support, and constructive ideas of many people. I owe a debt of gratitude to many of my clients and colleagues who suggested that it be written. The members of my personal staff have earned a special thanks. In particular, I wish to express my appreciation to Larry Spears and Dan Pollock for their editorial direction throughout the project.

HOW TO OWN YOUR OWN
PRIVATE INTERNATIONAL BANK

CHAPTER 1

INTRODUCTION

I have a confession. Whenever I start discussing my favorite topic, offshore finance, I can sound almost evangelistic. If I'm not extolling the blessings of global investing and the financial freedom that goes with it, I'm condemning, with equal parts sorrow and anger, the ongoing forfeiture of those financial blessings and freedoms in America.

And here's a further confession. I don't intend to lose that missionary zeal. In fact, the more I observe the vast financial harvests gained by my clients who move their money offshore, the greater the urgency and conviction I feel on the matter. (The case histories in chapter 7 are intended to provide "go-and-do-likewise" examples.) On the negative side, of course, I'm painfully aware that the penalties for financial inaction are growing heavier year by year.

Of course, I'm far from a lone voice crying in the financial wilderness. Increasing numbers of astute investment professionals have been joining the offshore chorus, counseling their clients to take advantage of the more liberal and enlightened laws of foreign money havens—nations that offer greater financial privacy, more wealth protection, and fewer taxes than does their home country. As a result, Americans, by the tens of thousands, have been investing their dollars, by the hundreds of billions, overseas.

Is it time for you to join this highly profitable exodus? To legally avoid taxes? To regain your privacy? To protect your assets? To invest internationally?

If your answer is not already a resounding yes, I certainly hope to change your mind before you've read very far in the pages ahead.

But that's just for openers. Marshalling the persuasive arguments for doing your banking offshore is only one aspect of this book. There is a further message that needs to be conveyed, a powerful financial strategy that is not for the average depositor or investor perhaps but that is ideally structured for individuals of high net worth.

That strategy, which is given short shrift or omitted altogether in most articles and books on money havens, is owning your own international bank. It may sound audacious, but it is, as you will see, both surprisingly doable and affordable. The advantages, for somewhat greater investment, are vastly greater rewards without commensurate risks.

But I'm getting ahead of myself. Let's back up a bit.

THE TROUBLE WITH ONSHORE BANKING

When I began consulting on international investment more than twenty-five years ago, I used to list all the serious shortcomings of the U.S. banking industry before launching into the offshore alternative.

Today I find that almost unnecessary. The people who come to my lectures or contact my office have already seen through those pillared porticos and marble lobbies. They know too well about the leaking money vaults and back-room shenanigans. Like the rest of us, they lived through the savings-and-loan (S&L) debacle of the 1980s, in which the U.S. government poured $160 billion (mostly borrowed) to clean up the thrift industry (with interest, the cost to tax-payers will be closer to $480 billion). And they're still living through the financial merger-mania of the 1990s, which has all but eliminated the neighborhood bank branch and flesh-and-blood tellers. They're tired of automated phone menus, where a live human voice is not a touch-tone option.

And just like you, I'll wager, the folks who seek out my advice have grown weary of the arrogance of most home-grown financial institutions, which couldn't care less about individual checking or savings accounts and which eagerly maximize fees while minimizing customer service and depositor interest. (And why not? These big banks stay in business only because of their investment portfolios any-way.) Some domestic credit-card issuers now charge customers a penalty for *not* using their cards for six months and an even steeper penalty if they decide to close the account. Others impose an annual fee on those who pay in full each month.

Actually, these scroogelike practices are small change compared to the real crippling defects of U.S. banks. I will detail many of these flaws in the chapters ahead. Most of them are due to massive federal intervention and overregu-lation, which in turn trace to Big Brotherly banking laws laid down during the Great Depression. But the nickel-and-diming of depositor accounts and credit-card balances is indicative of the panicky solutions the industry is adopting to its current crises.

The deepest crisis banks face, oddly enough, may not be strictly financial but one of identity. Ongoing deregulation has changed the rules of the money game. The sacred walls protecting banking's privileged precincts have been toppled. The result is an institutional free-for-all where thrifts,

The deepest crisis banks face, oddly enough, may not be strictly financial but one of identity. Ongoing deregulation has changed the rules of the money game. The sacred walls protecting banking's privileged precincts have been toppled. The result is an institutional free-for-all where thrifts, brokerage houses, insurance companies, credit unions, loan companies, and even retail chains are all fighting for pieces of the financial action.

brokerage houses, insurance companies, credit unions, loan companies, and even retail chains are all fighting for pieces of the financial action.

"We're trying to make a decision about what is a bank," lamented former Federal Reserve Board Chairman Paul Volcker a few years back.

If no one in America knows what banks *are* anymore, there is one thing we can say with certainty—and that is what these too-pompous institutions are *not*. They are not a safe place to deposit sizable chunks of money, especially not if you want to see that money grow.

But there are alternatives—an entire world of alternatives, in fact—beckoning just beyond our borders.

INTRODUCTION TO PRIVATE INTERNATIONAL BANKING

One investment principle is absolutely unarguable: the wisdom of diversification. But too few investment advisers take this principle to its logical conclusions. Diversification doesn't mean putting your portfolio eggs only in a variety of domestic baskets—stocks, bonds, mutuals, tax-exempts, money markets, real property, and so on. Real diversification means putting a basket or two in another country. The benefits of doing this, as you'll see, go far beyond mere asset protection. It's a financial strategy employed not only by resourceful and rugged individuals but also by America's largest corporations. For centuries, in fact, the smartest money has always gone looking for homes away from home, thereby increasing both safety and leverage.

Print and television journalists, as you may have noticed, have tried to equate "offshore banking" with "money laundering." Almost every media mention is followed by some reference to illegal tax havens, drug cartels, loot stashed by deposed dictators, and so on. This broadbrush condemnation of offshore centers as criminal hideaways is encouraged by domestic banks since it keeps average depositors from discovering how *they* could benefit from international banking; and it must delight the Internal Revenue Service (IRS), which has created a special arm of the Department of the Treasury specifically to stop the flight of capital across our borders.

Of course, illicit practices have flourished offshore, just as they have onshore, and I'll be discussing the various ways to steer well clear of them. The purpose of this book, after all, is to show you how to operate offshore legally to maximum effect. The fact is, despite the constant negative press (and the IRS strike force), more and more Americans, individual and corporate, are putting their money to work overseas. The number of people who use international private banking services has risen from eight million in 1984 to twenty million in 1997. Together, these enterprising folks constitute a multi-trillion-dollar industry! (By one estimate, nonresident Caribbean bank deposits alone exceeded $1 trillion. According to Shorex, which hosts an annual offshore exhibition and conference, the offshore industry is currently worth $5 trillion, making it the world's largest financial industry.) Banks in Switzerland, Austria, the Caribbean, the South Pacific, and elsewhere continue to be used by the most respected business names in the world for wholly legitimate purposes (creating wealth having not yet been outlawed!).

Stripped of mystique and misinformation, the offshore concept is easily conveyed. For the purposes of this book, offshore banking is simply banking, borrowing, or investing in countries other than the United States—*invariably countries with laws and regulations more favorable than those that apply in the United States.*

THE ADVANTAGES OF GLOBAL INVESTMENT

In 1997, the U.S. stock market continued its unprecedented bull run. Through November 21 of that year, the Dow Jones was up 22.22 percent, the Standard & Poor's (S&P) 500 index was up 30.02 percent, and the Nasdaq index of smaller stocks was up 25.54 percent. Meanwhile, the East Asian economic "miracle" slammed into sudden reverse, sending stock markets and currencies from Korea to Malaysia into financial freefall.

Moral of the story: Keep your money in the good old U.S.A., right?

Wrong. Even with the Asian calamities, foreign stock markets outperformed U.S. markets in 1997—one of Wall Street's recent banner years! Here are eighteen other world markets that, through November 21, provided returns higher than the S&P 500's 30.02 percent growth in 1997:

The chief lesson of these amazing figures? Go ahead and invest in America if you wish, but put a sizable portion of your wealth to work overseas. These international markets allow you to make money anytime of the day or night, free of the red tape that has continued to stifle U.S. markets and without excessive taxation. The unfortunate truth is that, while the United States has done little to modernize its investment structure, other countries have been busy passing laws to encourage new and creative financial products.

Country	Percentage Up*
Turkey	215.27%
Colombia	66.88%
Portugal	59.83%
Greece	54.13%
Switzerland	45.24%
Italy	45.23%
Mexico	43.77%
Finland	42.89%
Denmark	40.77%
Venezuela	39.66%
Netherlands	38.62%
Ireland	37.26%
Germany	36.46%
Spain	34.00%
Brazil	33.84%
Sweden	32.96%
Israel	32.65%
Chile	30.33%

*All percentages calculated in local currencies, not dollar conversions.

This is one reason so many financial forecasters continue to believe that the lion's share of money to be made by individual Americans over the next several decades will be made abroad. Offshore investments already attract more American capital than onshore investments. And, according to President Clinton's undersecretary of commerce, Jeffrey E. Garten, nearly 75 percent of the overall growth in world trade during the next two decades will take place in developing countries. "These emerging markets are likely to double their share of the world GDP in that time," he reports. "By the year 2010, their share of world imports is likely to exceed that of Japan and the European Union combined."

As we approach the end of the twentieth century, the age of global investment is already upon us. In 1970, U.S. equities constituted fully two-thirds of the world's stock market. In 1997, less than one-third were American. In only a few short years, the equation has shifted dramatically. Nearly 70 percent of the world's stocks (and more than 55 percent of its fixed income) is already invested in overseas markets. It makes little sense, obviously, to limit your investing sphere to just the United States.

I sometimes think of the term *offshore* as a state of mind, a new way of seeing a new investment world—as one enormous economic system made up of various interdependent financial markets. Your assets are your entry tickets into one (or all) of these new world markets. The only real boundary is your imagination.

GOING OFFSHORE: THREE STEPS

After investigating the financial options that exist offshore and diversifying your portfolio, it's time to take action. It need not be a bold action. In fact, I strongly advise new clients *against* any initial high-stakes ventures requiring the offshore transfer of major assets. A modest approach is far more sensible. Your first step can be as simple as opening a bank account in a foreign country. From such a simple step, we will see, great things can follow.

1. Open an offshore account. There was a time, a few decades back, when doing your banking offshore could be slightly complicated. No longer. With high-tech telecommunications, an offshore bank might as well be your neighborhood branch (which probably doesn't exist anyway). Credit and debit cards provide instant access to your money. Computerized communications can automate transferring funds or paying bills or sending instructions from home, just like the electronic banking software being promoted by U.S. banks. If computer wizardry is out of your comfort zone, a fax machine will work fine—and almost as quickly. Standard offshore bank accounts are no more difficult or expensive to open than U.S. accounts. In fact, because of less government red tape, you may find the paperwork even less!

2. Establish your own private international bank. How you use the corporation is entirely up to you. You can, for instance, simply let it operate as your broker in the international marketplace, investing in stocks, commodities, CDs, real estate, or foreign currencies. Or it can import and export all around the world and serve as a holding company to protect patents and trademarks.

Must you personally run this offshore corporation? Absolutely not. Professional management services groups offer a full line of investment and administrative services as well as insurance for the tax-free status of the corporation. And working with one of these firms will make it clear to the IRS that your firm is truly a foreign entity and not just a paper corporation designed to avoid taxes.

3. Establish your own offshore bank. This will allow you to take the most advantage of the special banking privileges, tax laws, and financial regulations of the various international banking centers.

In my view, step 3 offers the ultimate in offshore money-making potential, and it will be the main focus of this book.

Private International Banks

Chartered under the laws of the countries in which they operate, such private banks are fully recognized by the international banking community. Even more important, they provide a wide range of services well beyond the legal capability of domestic U.S. banks.

But perhaps the most striking feature of owning a private international bank is this: It is a single investment yet a total financial strategy for both building and protecting wealth.

What Makes These Banks More Attractive?

It's not the exotic backdrop, as glorious as that can be, especially in the Caribbean and western Pacific. Nor is it the level of service, though you'll find most offshore banks still very attentive to their depositors, anxious to maintain your confidence—and your funds to invest. (And, of course, if *you* happen to own the bank, you can be certain of getting preferential treatment!)

No, the prime attraction is the fact, just alluded to, that these institutions are unaffected by the big-government viruses that have infected all U.S. banks—confiscatory taxation, red-tape strangulation, and unwarranted invasion of financial privacy.

Offshore banks were instituted, as were U.S. banks originally, in accordance with free-market economics and capital formation—the miraculous engines that created America's prosperity. Capital accumulation, entrepreneurship, and technological ingenuity remain the three keys to economic progress: Money must be saved and invested, and new technologies must be devised. Unfortunately, most Washington bureaucrats don't really believe in free-market capitalism, except as something to suppress. Savings, investment, and ingenuity, they seem to believe, should be levied to the limit at every stage.

Ironically, then, it is these entrepreneurial banks all over the globe that are keeping faith with the original free-market American dream, a dream all but abandoned at home. An argument could even be made that those who invest offshore are the real patriots.

It is hardly surprising that alert American corporations and individuals are continuing to avail themselves of these offshore money markets. Again and again, private international banks have proven to be uniquely beneficial for raising capital, reducing taxes, lowering loan costs, and ensuring complete privacy and confidentiality of one's business affairs.

As declared flatly by one offshore owner, "A private international bank is the most powerful business tool known today."

MAIN FEATURES OF TAX-ADVANTAGED INTERNATIONAL BANKING

The international banking centers with little or no taxes are largely concentrated in two geographic regions: the Caribbean and the Pacific. Switzerland, long considered the world's number-one money haven, has now slipped into the second tier of offshore financial centers. There are several reasons for this decline. The big Swiss banks have relaxed their secrecy laws while agreeing to close cooperation with U.S. tax authorities. The vaunted reputation of the "gnomes" of Zurich, meanwhile, has been tarnished by revelations that, during World War II, they not only purchased Nazi gold but also seized and held Jewish assets.

The main countries currently hosting tax-advantaged private international banks are Anguilla, Bahamas, the Cayman Islands, Grenada, the Netherlands Antilles, Barbados, Belize, Hong Kong, the Cook Islands, Western Samoa, British Virgin Islands, Turks and Caicos, Vanuatu, and Nauru. More nations are joining the ranks each year.

Note: The laws of various foreign centers differ greatly, and one jurisdiction may be more attractive than another at any given time, so careful current analysis is essential before selecting a bank locale.

Some of these IOFCs (international offshore financial centers) are small island nations with weak economies—and it's easy to see why. Small islands have fewer natural resources than industrialized countries and little industry to

Though the Caribbean Basin has become the hub of international banking activity, the Pacific-Asian area has boomed in recent years despite the return of Hong Kong to the People's Republic of China. There has been an explosion of smaller financial centers, such as Nauru, Vanuatu, the Cook Islands, and Tonga. If this rate of growth continues, the Pacific-Asian market may soon lead the world in international banking activity.

provide jobs for their inhabitants. With unemployment often high, the citizens are usually poor. By enacting banking secrecy laws and liberal tax laws, such countries can attract foreign capital. Investors from the United States, Europe, South America, and elsewhere pay an annual fee to operate their own banks. In turn, the islands' appeal as offshore financial centers attracts more money and tourism, increases employment, and enhances their stature and reputation within the international economic community.

To secure a niche in the highly competitive world of international commerce, island governments must tailor various aspects of their legal systems to accommodate international banking activities. As a result, these private international banks are able to do business tax free, without burdensome red-tape regulations and with complete privacy. These conditions offer tremendous competitive advantages to owners and customers alike.

Though the Caribbean Basin has become the hub of international banking activity, the Pacific-Asian area has boomed in recent years despite the return of Hong Kong to the People's Republic of China. There has been an explosion of smaller financial centers, such as Nauru, Vanuatu, the Cook Islands, and Tonga. If this rate of growth continues, the Pacific-Asian market may soon lead the world in international banking activity.

WHO'S WHO IN OFFSHORE BANKING?

As mentioned, one of the media-made myths regarding offshore banking is that, since it has been used by money launderers and tax evaders, the entire industry is disreputable, if not actually illegal. Nothing could be farther from the truth. If offshore banking is to be judged by the company it keeps, the list of references is gilt-edged. Some of the most prestigious U.S. corporations have major international banking concerns, among them Pfizer Inc., American Express, Merrill Lynch & Co., and the country's largest financial services firm, American International Group (AIG).

The profit potentials of private international banking took on sudden significance to American corporations back in 1969, when the Federal Reserve imposed a 10 percent reserve requirement on banks. In plainer terms, this placed a limit on the amount of money an American corporation could pump into foreign subsidiaries or borrow from offshore sources.

At the same time, a good deal of money for domestic ventures was available only from European sources. This was due to the huge dollar reserves the major European countries and Japan had accumulated as a result of the U.S. balance-of-payments deficits. In order to tap the multibillion-dollar Eurodollar market for financing domestic operations, many multinational corporations were virtually forced to establish their own affiliated banking subsidiaries. This they did—at first in Switzerland and later in offshore havens around the globe.

In consequence, these U.S.-based multinationals found they could conduct banking business and shift investments virtually tax free, exchange currency without restriction, and operate in an environment of complete secrecy and privacy. Most important, because this business was conducted internationally, they did not have to comply with meddlesome U.S. banking regulations.

This is why, even when the reserve requirements were lowered in 1974 and again in 1988, the international banking business continued to expand. Many corporate-owned international bank operations have evolved into complex configurations of foreign ownership that are the very pinnacle of financial leverage.

Pfizer's banking arm—Pfizer International Bank Europe (PIBE)—was organized in the Cayman Islands to help the company better manage its offshore capital flow. Later relocated to Ireland, PIBE reported net income for the years 1994, 1995, and 1996 of $33 million, $35 million, and $27 million respectively. PIBE's assets at the end of the 1996 fiscal year were $512 million.

American Express owns American Express International Banking Corp. (AEIB), based in London, with satellite offices in the Caymans, Hong Kong, and other locations. The AEIB is not used for domestic banking purposes, nor does it maintain offices in the United States (only a representative in New York). Despite this, AEIB has returned to its parent company an average net profit in excess of $30 million per year since the mid-1970s.

In addition, some of the best-known names in American commerce do their banking offshore: Sears, Boeing, Firestone, Continental Oil, Seagram, Exxon, Monsanto, Rockwell International, and Fluor are but a few. Bank of America, Chase Manhattan Bank, Citibank N.A., Chemical Bank of New York, The First National Bank of Chicago, and scores of other conventional banking institutions worldwide are part of this growing international community. Obviously, the

American banking industry enthusiastically supports off-shore banking—but only for itself, not you!

And, not surprisingly, many of America's wealthiest families and famous names in business, politics, entertainment, and athletics maintain foreign bank accounts or offshore trusts to protect and increase their personal fortunes. Current statistics indicate that about one in every four Americans earning over $100,000 a year now invests offshore.

So, far from being "disreputable," offshore banking continues to enhance its reputation with the participation of financial heavyweights. In 1970, for example, Bank of America earned 19 percent of its total income from non-U.S. sources. Ten years later, its overseas profits accounted for a hefty 50 percent of its annual earnings. That same year, Citibank earned nearly 75 percent of its money overseas. And the overseas banking revenues of both these financial giants continue to grow today.

IMPLICATIONS FOR ALL INVESTORS

The message is clear: Major banks and corporations are involved in offshore banking because it makes both money and sense. Their leadership should be a signal to individuals, medium-size companies, and investment consortiums that international banking is a sound, profitable business venture.

This means that, whatever your current financial considerations, private international banking can provide *you* with an investment strategy that is both practical and profitable. It can permit you to conduct financial transactions in a secure environment, free of burdensome government rules and regulations. And, as an extra enticement, it offers entrée into the prestigious world of international finance.

> **O**nce you acquire your own international bank, you can operate according to your own priorities. You can lend to third parties, make private investments, accept deposits, initiate and administer trusts, purchase real estate at low interest rates, transfer currency at your discretion, offer customers back-to-back loans, acquire option/merger funding, and tap into escrow funds for short-term interest gains. In other words, you can fully compete for multi-million-dollar business with the world's major commercial banks.

And all these benefits accrue just to *depositors*. For *owners* of private international banks, the advantages are vastly magnified. I don't hesitate to say that the sum total is substantially greater than that offered by any other investment vehicle. Financial activities reserved only for banks—such as direct access to international capital markets, bank-to-bank benefits in the form of wholesale borrowing, and reduced foreign-exchange transaction fees—are instantly accessible to you, the individual, in your capacity as a bank owner or principal.

Once you acquire your own international bank, you can operate according to your own priorities. You can lend to third parties, make private investments, accept deposits, initiate and administer trusts, purchase real estate at low interest rates, transfer currency at your discretion, offer customers back-to-back loans, acquire option/merger funding, and tap into escrow funds for short-term interest gains. In other words, you can fully compete for multi-million-dollar business with the world's major commercial banks.

THE UNIQUE VALUE OF A PRIVATE INTERNATIONAL BANK

The phenomenal growth of private international banking has its source in the special benefits offered by these hosting havens. These include not only freedom from overregulation but also sound banking practices that can help you build your fortune while shielding it from government taxation and unscrupulous creditors.

Safety is always foremost. The myth, of course, is that offshore banking is too risky. The truth is just the opposite. Offshore institutions are safer than U.S. banks. Almost all offshore banks are self-insured, meaning every dollar on deposit must be backed by a dollar in liquid assets. The Federal Deposit Insurance Corporation (FDIC) requires U.S. banks to maintain only 10 percent liquidity. No other country has had as many bank failures as the United States.

Deposit insurance was triggered by bank failures of the Great Depression. For thirty years after the passage of deposit insurance, banks continued to defend themselves against funding risks by careful "asset management." But by the early 1960s, banks had turned to "liability management"—that is, by going into the money markets deliberately to buy what they would then lend—and ceased to concern themselves about funding risk. More and more frequently, then, from the mid-1970s through the early 1980s, the Federal Reserve was called on to supply funds to reckless banks because the market had closed on them. The full S&L crisis was upon us.

One of the culprits clearly was the rescue mind-set, which encouraged bankers to make less-than-prudent investments and loans. After all, FDIC-insured accounts have the option of being bailed out if they don't follow good management practices. Unfortunately, too many American banks are *not* well managed and, indeed, are operating at their worst performance levels since the Depression. Some audits have found many of the nation's major banks still with insufficient capital to support their business and hundreds of lesser banks on the brink of failure.

With the federal government chronically short of funds, a severe run on the banks would quickly deplete those inadequate FDIC reserves. Currently, the FDIC's Bank Insurance Fund hovers around $1.30 per $100 of insured deposits, or 1.3 percent. (The Federal Reserve actually considers this a "high" balance!) The Federal Savings and Loan Insurance Corporation (FSLIC) is in a similarly precarious position. The Savings Association Insurance Fund (SAIF), which insures deposits at thrifts, has only $.37 for every $100 of insured deposits—or only .37 percent of total deposits. (The FDIC chairman admits this is "significantly underfunded.")

What's really protecting those banks? Free-market economist and 1996 Libertarian presidential candidate Harry Browne has called it the "sticker principle": The government simply puts a sticker in the window of each bank saying that all accounts are protected by the FDIC. If that piece of paper actually convinces depositors their money is protected, then the sticker is technically "true."

As independent entities, without benefit of bail-out "voodoo economics," offshore banks must operate efficiently and economically, or they will fail. They don't have the option of falling back on inflated government promises. In addition, unlike the domestic banks, offshore institutions must maintain a higher ratio of liquidity, that is, the ratio of liquid assets to debts. Their reserve requirements are much higher than onshore banks. In sum, offshore banks are financially stronger, safer, and better managed as a whole than most domestic banks.

And, since these institutions tend to be free of costly regulations, they can offer a broader range of services to their customers and benefits to their owners. These include the following:

Profit.   All banks, foreign and domestic, borrow money from their depositors at a low rate and lend it out to borrowers at a higher rate. Private international bank owners not only collect money from depositors but also profit from opportunities of money manipulation available only to banks. Investors cite profit as their number-one reason for moving assets out of U.S. jurisdiction.

Privacy.   Strict banking secrecy laws of host countries shield records of financial institutions from unwarranted probes by government agencies, tax officials, legal claimants, aggressive business competitors—even ex-spouses. A private international bank ensures against financial intrusions that have become commonplace in domestic banking.

Tax protection.   International financial centers have earned a reputation as legal tax havens. Because host countries tax income of internationally licensed banks at a low rate—or have no taxes on them at all—a private international bank can shield its owner's dividends, interest, and royalties from IRS appropriation. This is why offshore havens have been called the "ultimate tax shelter."

Bank ownership with minimal red tape.   A private international bank can be owned at a surprisingly low cost. What's more, an international bank owner does not need a string of banking credentials. In most cases, past business experience is sufficient qualification, especially given the availability of low-cost, professional management companies to help the inexperienced bank owner.

Asset protection.   Assets placed in your own private international bank are immune to all judgments, seizures, and other judicial writs issued in the United States. Offshore asset protection provides considerably more protection than do conventional domestic asset protection strategies, such as titling assets in irrevocable trusts or family limited partnerships.

Asset diversification.   The best way to ensure the security of assets is to distribute them geographically. There is no better way to achieve such distribution than by placing them in one or more private international banks that you own and operate according to your personal specifications.

THE THREE P'S

Taken together, Profit, Privacy, and Protection constitute what I call the Three P's of offshore banking. In succeeding chapters, I examine each of these essential elements in detail, followed by a few inspiring case histories, to show exactly how others, from all walks of life and income levels, have prospered personally from the use of such banks.

Risk factors are assessed in chapter 8. While eminent advantages certainly exist in the offshore world, so do potential pitfalls. This chapter shows how to avoid or minimize them. The discussion is followed by a comparison of various private international banking centers in chapter 9 with an analysis and ranking of the fourteen most attractive offshore havens, comparing their geography, economics, politics, legal structure, and key features of interest to foreign investors. The book's final chapter walks you through typical steps in acquiring your own private international bank, with emphasis on selecting a qualified professional bank management company.

But we begin, in the next chapter, with a simple explanation of how a private international bank works.

CHAPTER 2

HOW A PRIVATE INTERNATIONAL BANK WORKS

PRINCIPLES OF OFFSHORE BANKING

The dictionary defines *offshore banking* as banking involving more than one country. Thus, from the U.S. perspective, offshore banking is simply banking outside the United States. If you were a French businessman, "offshore" could refer to a U.S. bank or a bank anywhere outside France.

For an offshore or foreign entity (e.g., a corporation or a bank) to avoid the application of U.S. laws, first, that entity must be organized under the laws of a foreign country. Second, it must not be "engaged in a trade or business" within the United States. Thus, to qualify for foreign treatment, offshore business needs to be conducted outside the United States.

To the degree an offshore company *does* do business in the United States, it may be subject to U.S. law. Complicating matters is the fact that an American individual or corporation owning 10 percent or more of an offshore entity may be subject to U.S. tax on the entity's undistributed earnings. Thus, to gain foreign treatment under U.S. tax, banking, and securities laws, American involvement with offshore entities must be planned and structured correctly. The easiest way to gain the greatest foreign benefits is through a private international bank. Private international banks are accorded special privileges by U.S. tax laws that make it possible to avoid the pitfalls ordinary foreign corporations face.

The mere existence of a foreign corporation, however, is not deemed conclusive proof that an enterprise is doing business outside the United States. The IRS, the Securities Exchange Commission (SEC), and banking regulators will sometimes challenge the integrity of a foreign company's foreign status. The legal test making a bank subject to U.S. law is whether it has "a sufficient nexus or connection with the U.S." What this vague terminology really means is that, in order to avoid confrontation with U.S. regulators, your private international bank should not deal with U.S. citizens or residents, advertise in the United States, or maintain banking offices there.

INTERNATIONAL MANAGEMENT COMPANIES

So how do you operate an offshore bank without your participation making it subject to U.S. tax and banking laws? The ideal solution is an international management company operating in a foreign jurisdiction.

International management companies fulfill an important role in the world of private international banking. Though not necessarily based in the country where the private bank is chartered, they provide a local presence (via agents or local officers or directors) in the foreign jurisdiction. As such, they can accomplish virtually any type of

A bank of this type is fully recognized in the international banking community. In fact, many prestigious private international banks operate in precisely this fashion through what is commonly known as a "letter box," identified by little more than a "brass plate." They don't need marble lobbies or gilded teller cages. They deal with their clients by mail, e-mail, fax, the Internet, or telephone or through agents situated outside the foreign jurisdiction.

transaction the parent owner of a private international bank wishes to undertake—from within the country where the bank is located.

The key component under U.S. law in determining offshore status is offshore management. Thus, with an offshore bank management company providing officers and directors delegated by the shareholders to manage the bank and conduct any business that may come before them, the private international bank qualifies as a foreign entity.

Of course, the management company must be qualified and experienced. It must be able to provide local officers and directors, handle day-to-day banking business, and keep accurate records of the bank's transactions.

It may be only a legal entity operating from a one-room office in a Caribbean city through a shared resident agent. No matter. A bank of this type is fully recognized in the international banking community. In fact, many prestigious private international banks operate in precisely this fashion through what is commonly known as a "letter box," identified by little more than a "brass plate." They don't need marble lobbies or gilded teller cages. They deal with their clients by mail, e-mail, fax, the Internet, or telephone or through agents situated outside the foreign jurisdiction.

However, private international banks do require financial sophistication if they are going to compete with other banks for business on an international scale, and top-flight professional management companies can provide that essential banking sophistication.

TRANSFERRING ASSETS AND MONEY OFFSHORE AND BACK INTO THE UNITED STATES

Most international banking transactions are "cashless," electronic bookkeeping entries that zip across borders on the wings of computers and telecommunications links. The movement of money between foreign centers typically involves such computer transfer, not physical receipt and delivery of currency. An international bank's funds are actually held in the bank's own deposit account with a commercial bank at one of the money centers. For U.S. investors, this usually means maintaining deposits with New York, Chicago, or Los Angeles banks. For European investors, funds are often held in London.

Assets such as real estate, securities, commodities, bullion, personal property, receivables, notes, and contracts may be placed in a private international bank in several ways. Assets and documents of title to assets do not have to be physically located internationally in order to be owned by the bank. The bank, like any corporation, has a distinct and separate legal personality. It is this foreign personality, not the location of the assets, that gives rise to the benefits.

Thus, the transfer of right, title, and interest in an asset to the bank's name moves that asset offshore, even if it's physically located in an office building on Sunset Boulevard in Los Angeles. (In most cases, the transfer of U.S. property that has an appreciated basis will trigger the imposition of an excise tax. However, with prudent tax planning, the excise levy may be legally avoided. For information on ways to transfer assets without alerting U.S. banking and taxing authorities, see chapter 4, "Privacy Benefits of a Private International Bank.")

If an asset is transferred outside the United States, it may be freely brought back into the country without tax consequence, provided it has not increased in value. If profits or gains are repatriated as income, dividends, interest, or capital gains, a tax is imposed on receipt. However, private international bank profits or gains that accumulate internationally and remain undistributed are untaxed—provided tax regulations are observed.

The two most common ways to use bank profits without tax consequences are through additional portfolio investment or by making loans in accordance with U.S. tax regulations and definitions of banking. (For further details on this, see chapter 5, "Tax Protection Benefits of a Private International Bank.")

FROM PRINCIPLE TO PRACTICE

Ever since the concept of private international banking began, freedom-seeking entrepreneurs have found different ways to use such banks. Here are a few examples:

Pfizer Inc.

As mentioned in chapter 1, Pfizer International Bank Europe (PIBE) is an Irish-chartered international bank owned by the pharmaceutical giant Pfizer Inc., based in New York City. As an aside, it might be noted that, as a Fortune 500 company, Pfizer would not be involved in offshore banking unless it knew it could have the full sanction of U.S. law.

Figure 2.1 shows part of Pfizer's 1997 10-K Report filed with the SEC. For the year 1996, PIBE reported a net income of $27 million. Here, in fine print, is a success story of a corporation that ostensibly maintains no U.S. banking interest but that has nonetheless (or for that very reason) ventured into the international banking business and produced a highly profitable return.

American International Group

American International Group (AIG) is America's largest financial services firm—and clearly intent on getting even larger. In late December 1997, New York–based AIG agreed to pay $2.2 billion to acquire American Bankers Insurance Group Inc. in order to enter the credit insurance business. That's a hefty price tag, but obviously it is affordable to AIG, which, in 1996 alone, collected $2.5 billion in premiums.

The AIG's 10-K filings for 1996 show that one of its many financial subsidiaries is UeberseeBank AG (Overseas Bank), which "operates as a Swiss bank."

Merrill Lynch & Co.

Wall Street brokerage giant Merrill Lynch states in its 1996 10-K SEC filings that it "provides investment, financing, insurance and related services on a global basis." One of those unspecified "related services" happens to be international banking, through a subsidiary, Merrill Lynch International Bank Limited (MLIB Limited), a United Kingdom–chartered bank with branch offices in Germany, Singapore, Bahrain, Luxembourg, and Italy.

Another subsidiary, Merrill Lynch Bank (Suisse) S.A., a Swiss bank, provides a variety of services, including "individual client services to international private banking

SECURITIES AND EXCHANGE COMMISSION
Washington, D.C. 20549

FORM 10 - K

ANNUAL REPORT PURSUANT TO SECTION 13 OR 15 (d)
OF THE SECURITIES EXCHANGE ACT OF 1934

For the fiscal year ended December 31, 1996   Commission file number 1-3619

PFIZER INC.

(exact name of registrant as specified in its charter)

Corporate/Financial Subsidiaries

The Company conducts international banking operations through a subsidiary, Pfizer International Bank Europe ("PIBE"), based in Dublin Ireland. PIBE, incorporated under the laws of Ireland, operates under a banking license from the Central Bank of Ireland. it makes loans and accepts deposits in a number of currencies in international markets. PIBE is an active Euromarket lender through its portfolio of loans and

Banking Operation

The company's international banking operation, Pfizer international Bank Europe (PIBE), operates under a full banking license from the Central Bank of Ireland. PIBE extends credit to financially strong borrowers largely through U.S. dollar loans made primarily for the short and medium term, with floating interest rates. Generally, loans are made on an unsecured basis. When deemed appropriate, guarantees and certain covenants may be obtained as a condition to the extension of credit. To reduce credit risk, PIBE has established credit approval guidelines, borrowing limits and monitoring procedures. Credit risk is further reduced through an active policy of diversification with respect to borrower, industry and geographic location. PIBE continues to have S&F's highest short-term rating of A1+

Financial Subsidiaries

Combined financial data/segment information as of November 30, 1996, 1995 and 1994 applicable to the Company's financial subsidiaries, consisting of Pfizer International Bank Europe (PIBE) and a small captive insurance company, were as follows:

Condensed Balance Sheet (millions of dollars)	1996	1995	1994
Cash and interest-bearing Deposits	$ 78	$ 13	$ 285
Eurosecurities and securities purchased under resale agreements	45	34	4
Loans, net	381	433	767
Other Assets	8	8	13
Total assets	$512	$488	$1,069
Certificates of deposit and other liabilities	$ 87	$85	$ 198
Shareholder's equity	425	403	871
Total liabilities and shareholders' equity	$512	$488	$1,069

Condensed Statement of Income (millions of dollars)	1996	1995	1994
Interest income	$ 28	$ 44	$ 49
Interest expense	(3)	(3)	(4)
Other income/(expense) net	2	(6)	(12)
Net income	$ 27	$ 35	$33

The 1995 data reflect a reduction in PIBE's loan portfolio to bring PIBE's balance sheet into line with its business needs. PIBE continues to have S&F's highest short-term rating of A1+.

Figure 2.1.   Portion of Pfizer's 1997 10-K report

clients." Yet another banking subsidiary, ML Capital Markets Bank, headquartered in Ireland with branch offices in Germany, Milan, and Tokyo, specializes in currency transactions.

Combined foreign operations, again according to SEC filings, accounted for 30 percent of Merrill Lynch's global revenues in 1996.

AN EXAMPLE OF BANK PERFORMANCE

The case histories in chapter 7 show what several international banks have actually done for their owners. But here is a brief overview of the types of things that are possible when you own a private international bank. The financial possibilities, as you'll see, are virtually limitless.

For starters, as a bank owner you'll enjoy all the customer benefits associated with offshore banking without paying a thing because you'll be servicing yourself. You'll also gain a new level of financial privacy since much of what you transact will be processed in the bank's name rather than in your own.

There are other, more sophisticated profit perks. For example, all banks—foreign and domestic—borrow money from depositors. When you open a checking account at any commercial bank, you're really loaning that institution your money in exchange for a checkbook. Currently, U.S. banks are paying around 3.5 percent interest on checking accounts. Just to break even, banks must earn at least that much in investment return on your initial deposit. But banks, of course, are in business to make a profit. Typically, they do this by loaning your money out at the prime lending rate (by the end of 1997 that was around 9.5 percent, depending on the borrower and the situation) and pocketing the difference as profit.

Your private international bank can operate in the same fashion—accepting deposits and making loans—and, what's more, make money from both transactions. You earn a little from your depositors' money and a little more from borrowers.

Once you acquire enough depositors, your bank can issue letters of credit and financial guarantees if borrowers deposit a fixed sum of money for a specified period of time (usually ten years). The interest on that deposit is paid into a "sinking fund" that enables the bank to issue guarantees amounting to the deposit plus interest to the borrower.

You profit from this in three ways. First, your bank charges a nominal fee to issue the letter of commitment. Second, it charges several percentage points to issue the loan guarantee. Third, it gains the use of the client's secured deposit for the guaranteed period of time. If the borrower lacks sufficient capital for the initial deposit, your bank can lend him the money at a higher rate of interest than it pays to establish the sinking fund. Or, if the loan is obtained from a third party, your bank can charge an additional handling fee (in which case you can make money a fourth way).

Your offshore bank charter also permits you to provide back-to-back loans. In this fairly common transaction, funds deposited by one corporate subsidiary are used as collateral for a loan to another subsidiary of the same parent company. This allows diversified corporations to transfer their profits from one business arm to another—usually from a high-tax base of operation to a low-tax jurisdiction. When the parent company owns the offshore bank, the profit incentive is even more compelling because all handling costs and percentage-point charges are within a kind of revolving money door.

Finally, your offshore bank can offer secured lending. The most frequently issued loans are for venture-capital, high-risk projects involving high interest rates. Banking laws in the United States restrict lending activity at extremely high interest rates. Private offshore banks, however, are not subject to these restrictions. They can lend at whatever the free market will allow, sometimes 10 percentage points higher than loans made by conventional lenders.

Raising Capital

Assume you own Commerce Bank Ltd. (CBL), located in one of the leading offshore havens and managed by a qualified bank management company based in Canada. You are an adviser as well as sole shareholder. As an adviser, you are able to steer business to the bank without running afoul of state or federal banking laws. As a shareholder, you are able to direct the actual business of the bank.

Throughout history, banks have been considered pillars of the community. This reverent regard for banks continues today, even with the failures and bailouts and without regard for liquidity, assets, reserves, the quality of the loan portfolio, and any other critical factors. This Rock-of-Gibraltar image works to the advantage of private international banks, which, simply because they are banks, can often attract capital as easily as their domestic counterparts simply by asking for it.

As an example: You are at a party where several reasonably well-heeled people are enjoying food and drink. You spot author Bill Shakespeare, who knows a great deal about writing but little about banking. You start making small talk and gradually steer the conversation to matters of finance. At the proper moment, you mention your affiliation with an overseas bank that is currently paying 10 percent on one-year international certificates of deposit (CDs).

Shakespeare spills his martini. He is only getting 6.5 percent on his $100,000 CD at a local bank. Thinking himself a smooth financial operator, he decides (with some subtle prodding by you) that CBL should have the honor of being his banker. Immediately, he puts his hundred grand on deposit with you. That your bank is small is of little concern to him. It is a bank, and, as far as he knows, all banks are created equal. This transaction has accomplished the following:

For your bank:

1. You have raised $100,000 quickly and with little effort.
2. There is now an additional $100,000 available to you for portfolio investments.
3. Little expense was incurred in obtaining this money. Your cocktail-party solicitation was legal because you engaged in a private, not a public, offering.
4. The credibility of the bank has been enhanced by the addition of another person to the list of depositors.

   For the customer:

1. He will earn more on his money than he could from a domestic bank.
2. He now has a financial instrument that he can sell should he need liquidity.

Your Bank As Fudiciary

Commerce Bank can act as a middleman—a fiduciary—and make plenty of money doing so. But you must be careful. Timing is critical, or, as Shakespeare might say, "the readiness is all."

You can't arrange a deal and, once finalized, buy an international bank and reap the harvest. To maximize your profit on a major financial deal, you must own the bank before the deal making begins.

If you earn a commission for arranging a deal, you must pay tax on this to the IRS. The commission is ordinary income. If you arrange the deal and purchase the bank just before it is complete, the IRS may say that you were acting primarily on your own behalf and not as an agent for the bank. If, however, you have arranged the deal while working as an agent for the bank, and the bank earns the commission, the income is the bank's and is thus tax exempt.

To act as an international fiduciary and receive, hold, and disburse funds on behalf of third parties, you must operate CBL in an offshore haven and have an operating agreement with an international bank management company. (And as the owner of a private international bank, you'll have become exactly the kind of individual those with significant amounts of money might seek out to arrange a major deal.)

Your Bank As Loan Agency

You decide to hire agents to work on behalf of CBL, putting together loan deals for it—and, by the way, paying you for the privilege.

So you place an ad in the *Wall Street Journal*. You can advertise for agents there because you are looking for personnel. This is different from advertising your bank as such. You do not, however, advertise for salespeople. Your ad is in the Business Opportunities section, offering to license loan agents.

What are you licensing? The use of your bank's good name. In theory, anyone can be a finder and put together lender and borrower. In practice, few individuals have the clout to pull this off. That is why most major deals are put together by banks.

That's where CBL comes in. It licenses the person as a loan production agent. You charge him a one-time license fee of, say, $5,000 plus 10 percent of his gross. This is similar to a franchise arrangement, whereby the franchiser charges a one-time franchise fee and a predetermined royalty on sales.

Because CBL is an international bank, the loan production agent cannot operate in the United States. (There are exceptions, as in arranging mortgage loans in California.) Yet the loan production agent gets to use the bank's name, which will enable him to arrange far more deals than if he were on his own. He makes money from commitment and finder's fees. This transaction has accomplished the following:

For your bank:

1. It brought you representation at virtually no cost.
2. It earned CBL a $5,000 fee, up front, for every agent licensed.
3. It earned CBL 10 percent of each agent's gross.
4. If the loans are arranged so that they are back to back (borrower places funds in your bank as collateral for the loan), it increases your bank's capital.
5. It earned your bank the interest paid on the loans.
6. It increased CBL's exposure and name recognition.

For the agent:

1. It earned him credibility, which should substantially improve his ability to arrange deals.
2. It earned him fees for his services.

A Private International Bank Model

Following is a step-by-step scenario of how a private international bank might progress from idea to initial operation and on to full service.

Let's say CBL has a resident agent, foreign directors to manage it, a mailing address in the offshore haven, and an account at a commercial bank in Los Angeles, where you, the owner, happen to live. You are the sole signatory on that account. Your official connection with the bank, mandated by the minutes of CBL, is independent agent or adviser.

You make real estate, securities, and commodities investments and use the bank to reduce taxes on those portfolio investments—and on income from profits earned as a limited partner in a Hollywood movie.

As mentioned, you also raise capital from third parties in the form of deposits, which strengthens your contention that CBL is in the banking business, a crucial point for U.S. tax purposes.

That capital in the form of deposits may, within the limits of ordinary liability, be used to increase the size of your portfolio investments, even as CBL is obligated only to repay a fixed rate of return to depositors. Those depositors, meanwhile, are also potential customers to whom you can offer other banking services in the future.

Commerce Bank Ltd. has foreign directors in order to preserve the benefits of doing business internationally. It has an offshore mailing address, which is essential for securing business through advertisements placed in international media. And it has a commercial bank account in Los Angeles so that any deposit you acquire for CBL may be invested quickly, electronically, and internationally at your sole discretion.

However, it is not essential that you personally oversee all new bank business and decide what types of investments are appropriate for CBL. An attorney, accountant, or other person situated in the United States may take that position without creating tax problems for you, provided the attorney works for CBL, not for you personally.

Soliciting Customers

You can advertise on your World Wide Web home page, openly soliciting depositors. As the Internet is considered a transnational communication medium, it is wholly outside U.S. jurisdiction, so this solicitation does not infringe on U.S. tax or banking statutes. On its home page, CBL offers 10 percent per annum, tax free, on one-year CDs. The page directs prospective customers to write to either CBL's offshore address or its electronic mail address for further details. The resident agent for CBL's Canadian management company fulfills these requests, whether by s-mail ("snail mail") or e-mail, by sending prospective customers an account application and a letter describing CBL's CDs.

The ad and follow-up mailing is successful. Checks arrive at CBL's offshore post office box and are then remailed to the management company in Canada, where they are deposited in a Canadian bank. When the checks clear, CBL's management company or its resident agent confirms the deposit and sends the customer a CD in accordance with prearranged instructions from you.

One depositor lives in Chile and is most desirous of getting his money out of the country for fear of government expropriation. He sends a check for U.S.$5,000 for a one-year CD. The bank's management company deposits the check for collection in its Chilean correspondent bank. After collection, the U.S.$5,000 is wired to your account in Los Angeles and journaled as a loan on CBL's ledgers both internationally and in Los Angeles. It is then invested by you in securities, commodities, or real estate—at your discretion as CBL adviser.

The more this type of transaction occurs, the more quickly CBL will build assets and a solid customer list it can use in the future.

Providing International Banking Services

Some of your customers have expressed an interest in investment advice. You prepare a fifteen-page brochure describing the investment services CBL offers. These include safe deposit, investment advice on a performance-fee basis, trust services the government of the offshore haven has licensed it to perform, portfolio investment in CBL's name, precious-metals trading, and such other services as may develop into profit centers for CBL.

You have the brochures printed in Los Angeles and airfreighted to CBL's management company in Canada for mailing to your current and prospective customer lists. Numerous inquiries result from the mailing. They are forwarded by the management company's agent in the offshore financial center to CBL's adviser—you—in Los Angeles.

Some inquiries are handled by you by means of form letters and application blanks. Where interest is expressed by those of substantial means, you write a letter on CBL's stationery, signed by its resident agent, in which CBL agrees to entertain a meeting to discuss the needs of the bank's prospective clients. As a result of assured business, you as bank agent tour overseas, meeting with some of your clients. Extensive business develops.

Both you and CBL are unaffected by U.S. regulations since your customers are not residents of the United States. At this point, and in selected situations, you can begin filtering in U.S. customers developed through indirect contacts.

Servicing Your Own Needs

As any U.S. tax benefit you claim will be based on the contention that CBL is truly in the banking business, it is important that CBL actually acquire a mixture of customers—depositors, borrowers, and recipients of investment advice. Some are American, others are foreign residents.

Now you deposit some of your own capital into CBL, which uses it to make securities, commodities, and portfolio investments on your behalf. By acting as CBL's agent and adviser, you keep the income generated by investments on deposit with CBL, legally avoiding U.S. tax on it. CBL makes several loans to you, which are repaid within one year.

You also avail yourself of the tax-saving benefits and profit-making activities associated with the ownership of CBL.

Marketing

There are many methods a private international bank can use to acquire customers. The most obvious way to lure customers away from domestic commercial banks is by providing similar services at better prices, more efficiently, and on a more personalized basis.

For example, most American financial institutions provide letters of introduction, safe-deposit services, letters of credit, short-term financing, letters of commitment, trust services, collections, and similar activities. A private international bank can offer these or even more extensive services at perhaps a lower cost and, in many cases, more efficiently than commercial banks. However, it is important for the banker to fully understand how a private international bank may and may not get customers as well as how it may and may not serve them.

Because the federal government does not want to encourage its citizens to move their money out of the country, the extent to which international banks may solicit business from Americans is severely restricted. For example, CBL may not advertise its services publicly in the United States. It may not make a public offering in the manner of a publicly held corporation. However, international advertising is permitted by some offshore jurisdictions as are private, or so-called restricted, offerings.

As a worldwide medium, the Internet provides an excellent way to attract non-American individuals and companies as bank patrons. There is a significant need by wealthy investors around the world to invest in U.S. securities and real estate. Private international bankers are in a good position to tap this market by simply running an ad for the service or traveling abroad and making personal contact with prospects.

International banking ads are permitted over the Internet since, as mentioned above, this medium is regarded as

As a worldwide medium, the Internet provides an excellent way to attract non-American individuals and companies as bank patrons. There is a significant need by wealthy investors around the world to invest in U.S. securities and real estate. Private international bankers are in a good position to tap this market by simply running an ad for the service or traveling abroad and making personal contact with prospects.

basically "borderless," though there is obviously massive access within the United States. Besides worldwide penetration, another obvious advantage to the Internet is cost. The only expenses involved are in creating and maintaining an attractive and informative Web page, then getting it listed with major search engines. Not surprisingly, thus, you'll find an explosion of Web sites offering not only offshore banking services but also bank management and consulting services (see figure 2.2).

Private Offerings

A restricted, or private, offering is another permissible way of advertising for a bank—and it can be done in the United States as well as abroad. It usually takes the form of a personal, controlled contact, such as the example given earlier of a cocktail-party conversation that leads a customer to a private international bank. However, if an international banker were to advertise a cocktail party in the local newspaper and use the party to pitch his concept, he would be on shaky legal ground.

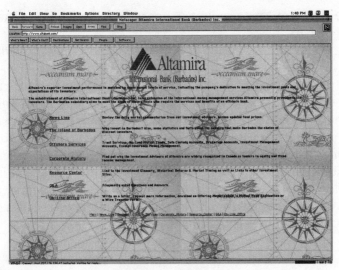

Figure 2.2. Web site http://www.altabank.com for Altamira International Bank (Barbados) Inc.

A private international banker or his agent may take part in investment seminars, speaking engagements, or other gatherings limited to selected individuals. General interest articles on the subject of international banks may appear in any media. This constitutes editorial content rather than paid advertising and may encourage an individual or business to place funds in the international banking system.

Solicitation through investment clubs or organizations may also prove successful. The goal of a private international bank's marketing program in this regard would be to explain such advantages to those with influence over the group.

Friends, fellow investors, existing business clients, associates, and other contacts are all potential customers of private international banks, if privately approached. The ingredients that make these marketing ventures pay off for the bank are the right promotional strategy and the right banking product. What makes them legal is their exclusivity.

Seen in this way, what first seems like a marketing disadvantage—restricted access to potential customers—is actually an asset. One of the primary concerns of private international banks is managing their financial affairs discreetly. What a private international bank might gain in broadening its customer base by advertising in the *New York Times* it would lose in privacy. The more visible a financial institution, the more vulnerable it is to attack by regulators. Where big domestic banks must take on customers more or less at random, the private international bank can screen its customers before extending them its services.

TOOLS OF THE TRADE

The explosive growth in offshore finance has been made possible by new technology. Thanks to sophisticated telecommunications and computerized banking services worldwide, money can be made, spent, won, lost, and transferred faster than ever before. And these same high-tech tools make establishing and operating a private international bank easier than ever before. A qualified bank-management service can help you put these systems into place—and help you hire good people to run them.

Electronic Communication

Just as personal contact is the essence of obtaining customers for a private international bank, electronic contact is the bank's means of serving them. When evaluating the potential of a given country to host a bank, the would-be owner should assess its accessibility to the United States—in physical terms and in terms of telecommunications. Both instant phone service and the availability of direct flights from an American city to the foreign jurisdiction are crucial factors that might determine the success or failure of a business deal.

Several years ago, a telex was essential for running offshore banking operations. Today, you might use one of these antiques as an extra boat anchor. What an international bank does need, in terms of electronic equipment, is an Internet-connected computer, a fax machine, a copier, and a reliable phone system.

This consists of a long-distance carrier, local phone companies in the United States, and a corresponding system in the host jurisdiction. Usage rates vary constantly, but at this writing an international phone call to the Caribbean or Pacific-Asian areas costs about $5.50 for three minutes.

Travel expenses must be considered an expense of private international banking since certain business activities (a closing ceremony, transfer of funds, or letter-of-credit relay) may require visiting the host offices. In such a case, travel and accommodation expenses become a part of the bank's income statement. If your bank is located on an island accessible only by sea canoe, your credibility as a banker might be suspect.

Bank Management Services

Considering that new owners of private banks may lack banking experience, it becomes useful to contract with a bank management company. In fact, few things have greater impact on the degree of success enjoyed by a private international bank than the management service. A good management service can perform all the significant administrative functions for a bank owner and recommend ways to make the highest possible profit and reap the most benefits from bank ownership.

For as little as $2,500 annually, a bank management firm will handle all your mail, telephone, fax, and computer communications; process deposits; and keep track of receipts. It will maintain your bank office, provide typing and photocopying service, and keep up your bank's files. It will draft key documents or deposit agreements, send out bills and statements, handle funds transfers to and from the United States, and act as custodian of your confidential records, documents, minutes, books, and ledgers—ensuring the privacy of your business dealings.

Even more important, a good management company can give you foreign-exchange privileges and access to wholesale capital markets. Such a company can also provide specific and sophisticated international investment advice whenever you need it.

However, as will be discussed in chapter 10, even before selecting a management company, you should consider selecting an offshore adviser. This should be a consultant knowledgeable about international investments—one who can tailor an overall offshore strategy to your individual needs. He or she will also be invaluable in weighing the accounting, tax, and legal issues involved in various offshore options.

Personnel

Besides a management firm, your operating statement must allocate resources to any secretarial, clerical, legal, or executive personnel necessary for running the bank. Depending upon the nature and scope of your particular strategy, you may want to hire them on a per-hour (or freelance) basis rather than as full-time employees. This is another area in which a professional consultant can offer guidance.

As already indicated, the easiest way to handle day-to-day operations is to have a qualified bank management company take care of everything—making the arrangements, hiring the people, and sending your bank a single bill for services.

Putting It All on Paper

Stationery, stock certificates, CD forms, application blanks, corporate minutes, letters of credit, and banking forms of all descriptions must be budgeted in a start-up operation.

This involves working with printers and graphic artists. It does not matter whether all printing is done in the United States. Since marketing and customer contact will take place by mail, there will also be an ongoing need to update printed promotional material, letters of introduction, and so on. For Internet marketing, a Web page designer will be needed.

Here again, a qualified bank management company can save considerable expense by using its expertise to identify and provide all necessary items.

If your bank intends to operate a high-volume business, a fully equipped business office in the United States will probably be a necessary expense, either out of your home or place of business (in the latter case, the "workstation" must be dedicated strictly to offshore interests). There is no restriction on operating a domestic office that performs solely clerical, secretarial, and administrative support services such as typing, bookkeeping, or relaying information from clients to the host country or bank management offices.

With a computer, modem, fax machine, and photocopier, you'll be able to create a virtual electronic control center, allowing you to operate day and night. Fancy desks and executive chairs are unnecessary. The money can be better invested in a tasteful brochure or promotional literature. Make sure your printed material is design coordinated. This makes it easier for investors, depositors, shareholders, and customers to identify your service or product. In business, consistency conveys stability.

It's also crucial to the success of your business that you project a strong, clear image and that you keep that image in front of those you want to impress. That image should be mirrored in everything from the design of your business cards to your Web page (if you have one) to the wording of any printed material outlining your offerings, products, or services.

And you should establish that image *before* you go off-shore. What will you call your bank? What logo will enhance that name? How will it look on stationery, services brochures, and various banking forms? What kind of customers will that image attract? Give serious thought to your prime markets and direct your choices toward their concerns and priorities.

A point on writing style: Straightforward letters and memos are the key to successful business writing. Make sure professional titles translate correctly. Clarify all written items having to do with money amounts. Be sure currency differences and rate exchanges are taken into account.

Legwork

Assembling the elements of a duly chartered private international bank involves a good deal of organization. Apart from the financial investment, you must be able to follow proper procedure and know how to shepherd a proposal through a bureaucracy—even the limited bureaucracies found in most countries that welcome private bankers.

Nonprofessionals who have chartered private banks without assistance report a time lag of six months to a year from initial investigation to first business day, depending on the host country. That can be a real problem since time and money are the key ingredients of successful international bank licensing.

That is where competent professional advisers come in. By using a qualified adviser with established connections in leading offshore havens, the astute investor can reduce the start-up time to less than two months—and reduce the usual aggravations tenfold. This time will be spent with initial consultations and planning; making the necessary equipment, personnel, and legal arrangements to license the bank; and conducting a background check on the prospective investor in order to indemnify the host country against any unsuitability of the prospective owner. Once the investigation is complete, relevant papers are filed with the foreign government—and the bank is in business.

This, of course, is only the beginning. The following chapters explore in greater detail the many prestigious benefits available to owners of a private international bank.

CHAPTER 3

PROFIT BENEFITS OF A PRIVATE INTERNATIONAL BANK

The essence of earning a profit in the banking business is borrowing money at a low rate of interest and lending it at a higher one. Yet the way banks borrow money is different from the way most corporations borrow. Banks borrow from their customers. The money deposited by one set of customers is in turn loaned out to another set. The difference between the amount the bank pays the first set of customers and the interest it collects from the second set is its ordinary profit.

In addition, the term *profit* refers to the spread between the cost of doing business and any income generated as a result of doing business. Cost reduction leads to increased profitability in any business. Private international banking is no exception.

For these reasons, the ability to borrow funds at a lower interest rate, to save on U.S. taxes, to save on transaction fees, and to operate at a lower cost than domestic banks all amount to savings, which can equate to new profits.

Anyone who opens a checking account at a commercial bank is really lending that bank his money in exchange for the privilege of having a checkbook. Since the early 1980s, banks have been paying interest on checking accounts (provided the account holders maintain a minimum balance ranging anywhere from $500 to $5,000). The rates paid on these accounts obviously fluctuate, but most today are paying less than 3.5 percent—a rate similar to that paid on regular passbook savings accounts. The cost to the bank is that 3.5 percent plus the cost of processing checks and maintaining records on the accounts. Meanwhile, the bank lends the depositor's money to third parties at the prime lending rate (or more, depending on the type of loan), keeping the difference (usually a spread of 3 to 12 percentage points) as profit.

A private international bank can perform the same type of activity as commercial banks, but it has one problem: It is prohibited from advertising publicly in the United States to attract customers. How, then, can it earn money by conducting ordinary banking business?

The answer is that there are many ways in which private international banks can be used as reliable and continuous sources of legitimate profits.

An Overview of Private International Bank Profits

As mentioned, the spread between income and cost of doing business constitutes the profit for any business. There are significantly lower costs in international banking than in domestic banking, identified as follows:

- Offshore banks are not required to maintain reserves against depository liabilities.
- There are no FDIC fees.
- Offshore banks can avoid a wide range of minor but costly regulatory constraints faced by domestic banks.
- International banks are not required to allocate credit to certain borrowers at below-market rates.
- Offshore banks are not forced to purchase certain types of securities (such as government debt), and they are free to allocate their resources as they choose.
- There are no credit ceilings restricting international banks from going after profitable business.
- There are no official limits on interest rates that may be paid on time deposits (as was formerly the case in the United States), nor are there lending-rate ceilings (as there still are in many states).

A private international bank can generate income mainly in three ways:

1. By taking deposits
2. By extending credit
3. By investing

In other words, the private international bank profits by operating effectively as borrower, lender, and investor.

Deposits Raise Cash—and Lead to Profits

A major attraction of private international banks to investors, large and small, is the interest rates these banks are willing to pay long-term depositors. They have been known to pay interest as high as 20 to 25 percent per annum on deposits left on account for nine years. Even in the lower interest-rate environment of the late 1980s and early 1990s, some private international banks were offering depositors as much as 12 percent on deposits of just one year.

Internet Marketing Strategies

If you sit down at your computer to surf the Web and type "offshore banks" into any Internet search engine, you will discover some attractive international banking pages that advertise various services and investment products (see figure 3.1). Internet home pages such as these are fast becoming the cyber-equivalent of the pillared facade and ornate lobby through which private international banks can lure new depositors. Obviously, the marketing goal is to bring in direct deposits. But even when they don't, they can provide a valuable asset—a list of interested parties that can be targeted with further marketing devices.

For example, when visitors to your bank's home page respond to an e-mail invitation for further information without actually sending in deposits, your bank management service can mail or e-mail complete information packets about your bank to them. This reinforcement of the original ad will usually bring in further deposits.

However, the mere ability to raise large amounts of money in deposit form does not make a bank profitable. After all, deposits are considered liabilities (money owed to depositors) on a bank's financial statement. Private international banks profit because they can move the depositors' funds into high-yielding investments—such as the stock market, real estate, currencies, precious metals, commodities, trust deeds, factoring programs, and other leveraged assets—that can earn substantially more than what the banks must pay the depositors when they redeem their accounts. The difference between the yield the bank has

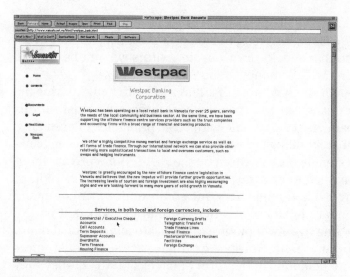

Figure 3.1.   Web site http://www.vanuatu.net.vu/html/
westpac_bank.html for Westpac Bank

received from its investment and the interest it must pay
the depositor is its profit.

Thus, most banks encourage their depositors to extend
the length of time they keep their money in the bank. The
longer a bank has principal available to it, the longer it can
continue to use that principal as seed money for investments
of its own, delaying the payback date of the principal
amount, if not the amount of yield.

WHY INTERNATIONAL BANK DEPOSITS ARE PROFITABLE

Though there is no reserve requirement for private international banks in most money havens, bankers are implicitly
liable for safekeeping all funds on deposit with them. In this
sense, cash reserves of a private international bank consist

of money available for business purposes. If the bank offers check-cashing services, obviously it must keep money available so that checks drawn by depositors will not be dishonored in the U.S. money system.

As the high number of failures of FDIC banks during the past decade attests, even the best-intentioned institutions and bankers have trouble with basic principles of cash flow. Fortunately, managerial incompetence in the domestic banking system is underwritten by the FDIC. But a private international banker cannot afford the visibility or discredit of having even a single account compromised. A command of standard business practices is thus an important part of protecting the profit picture of a private international bank.

In any bank, foreign or domestic, some customers execute demands in the form of checks on the money they earlier deposited while others make new deposits. Still others are repaying loans, which is a source of bank income. So the bank does not really need to keep a 100 percent cash reserve on hand in order to operate. A fractional reserve is all that is required.

In the area of constantly flowing demands and deposits, the international bank follows the custom of banks the world over in depending on the strong statistical probability that every depositor will not come in and call for his or her money at the same time and that every creditor will not call in loans (e.g., margin calls) owed by the bank.

Beyond the need to maintain a reserve against withdrawals, new deposits are important because they can be used in a number of ways to generate additional profits for the private international bank. Among the most commonly used methods are currency-exchange services and trust and cash management services.

Currency Exchange

A number of private international banks have taken advantage of the banking industry's ability to exchange currency for customers from a country whose currency is inconvertible in the normal marketplace. In a number of cases, private international banks have been successful in converting "troubled currencies" to U.S. dollars. The private international bank can legally maneuver around foreign-exchange restrictions because banks are typically immune to local currency restrictions—and, even though they are dealing in U.S. dollars, they can bypass any U.S. government sanctions because they are operating outside U.S. jurisdiction.

Because this type of transaction would be impossible by conventional means, the bank's fee in a situation of this type might be as high as 20 percent of the deposit—considerably more than the interest it would have to pay on the original deposit.

Trust and Cash Management Services

Trust company services may include the ability to receive assets into custody on behalf of clients and to manage, administer, and invest those assets in accordance with client instructions. Trust activities include the ability to act as trustee under deeds of settlement, wills, and other types of trusts—the same trust authority domestic banks exercise. The differences are that an international trust faces far less tax liability than its domestic counterpart and that investment options for the trust's assets are far more varied.

The bank's ability to profit in this way depends on the nature and extent of services involved and the diligence with which they are administered. Private international banks have charged from $5,000 to $10,000 per year to administer a trust for a client.

For an individual or a company, cash management means using otherwise dormant cash in the highest profit yielding situation obtainable. For example, an individual may choose to keep his cash in a high-yielding, cash-equivalent mutual fund with check-writing privileges (a so-called money market fund) rather than in an ordinary checking account.

The amount of yield necessary to attract funds in a given investment away from its next-best investment-yield situation is known as the "opportunity cost." For example, if a NOW checking account yields 3.5 percent per annum on average balances and a money market fund with check-writing privileges yields an annual rate of 6.0 percent, the difference in yield, or opportunity cost, is 2.5 percent per year. Expressed differently, it costs an investor 2.5 percent a year to keep his funds in a NOW account.

The need for cash management and lowest possible opportunity cost is more apparent in banking than in any other business. The objective of any banker is to ensure that his capital is invested in the highest-yielding opportunity legally available to him at any given time. For this reason, U.S. bankers would like to invest all their long-term deposits in high-yielding ventures such as commodities and real estate. However, they are specifically prohibited from doing so by federal banking law. International bankers, free of the Federal Reserve Board's restrictions, are able to invest all their capital—both long- and short-term—in any investment they feel is financially prudent. This is a primary reason that it is more desirable to own a private international bank rather than a U.S. bank.

Individuals and companies with large balances in their checking or savings accounts at commercial banks should also make decisions on the basis of the principle of opportunity cost. They would find it more profitable to maintain those balances with their own private international banks. Their bank may then make investments in any high-yield, acceptable-risk opportunity that presents itself—without regard to liquidity or reserve restrictions that would apply in the United States.

A private international bank is needed for this purpose in order to provide an element of separation between cash maintenance and investment opportunity. It may be imprudent for some corporations not to show cash in the bank on their balance sheet, even though all their cash may be invested wisely. The private international bank provides a way around this, allowing the parent corporation to show money on deposit in a bank while directing cash management investments with that money to earn profits and income free of local and U.S. taxes.

Corporations and individuals in the United States now experience a good deal of financial opportunity cost because they must maintain large balances at commercial banks for escrow accounts, trust accounts, real-estate broker accounts, travel-agent accounts, and insurance-broker accounts. In many situations, they could maintain these deposits in a private international bank. Because the international jurisdiction does not impose reserve requirements on the bank or its customers, they could have the bank make cash management investments appropriate to their needs, thus lowering their opportunity cost.

INSURANCE SERVICES

Many private international banks are providing insurance services to their customers. This may include various types of high-risk coverage, such as malpractice, corporate liability, strike, fire and flood, and insurance on other risks that would be too expensive to seek from ordinary underwriters. The ability to profit from providing these services depends largely on the competition of the market and the cost of the insurance if purchased from U.S. sources. The premiums add to the capital position of the bank, provide investment principal of the type used by U.S. insurance companies, and build up a reserve should any claims arise from the "captive" insurance operation. (*Captive insurance* is simply insurance with a company in the same group as the insured.)

The insurance business became a major profit center for many private international banks as a result of the liability crisis that hit U.S. companies, professionals, and even cities and counties in 1985. With domestic insurers charging outlandish premiums—or refusing to grant policies at all—those parties with high-risk positions had no alternative but to turn offshore. Some merely went to established foreign insurers willing to take on the risk at more reasonable premiums. Others, usually professional groups or individuals with common risks, established cooperative insurance pools that would provide coverage for all the members. Finally, many single companies, professional groups, and trade associations set up so-called captive self-insurance operations based in places like the Bahamas, Panama, or the South Pacific islands, where strict U.S. insurance regulations could be avoided and tax advantages gained.

For the insured parties, there are two immediate financial benefits in a captive insurance company. The first benefit is the mere fact that it can make certain types of coverage available. Conservative American underwriters still consider many ventures too risky and simply refuse to provide coverage or, if they can be talked into offering a policy, demand a premium that is prohibitive. Thus, a company that needs unconventional coverage before embarking on a new venture might have to abandon its plans because of the difficulty of finding a bond.

However, an international captive insurance plan, which can be reinsured by a conventional underwriter or by buying insurance from wholesalers with less difficulty, can solve the problem for many companies. Compared to the cost of initial coverage supplied by a domestic underwriter, the international premium is likely to be much lower. And, as reserves accumulate because of a low level of claims, the necessary level of reinsurance is reduced.

The second benefit is tax related, although the Tax Reform Act of 1986 wiped out much of this. Prior to that law, U.S.-based companies that self-insured through a captive offshore insurance company were able to pay their premiums into a contingency fund (set aside in case of trouble), invest that cash, return a tax-free dividend to policyholders if the investments did well—and still deduct the premiums as expenses on their U.S. tax returns.

However, the 1986 tax laws decreed that companies, as a general rule, can no longer deduct premiums paid to their own self-insurance subsidiaries and that all profits (including investment gains) made by the insurance subsidiary are taxable, even if those profits are not distributed to the parent firm or owners group. (The exception to this rule involves "mutual" insurance companies: those owned by 10 or more unrelated parties. Tax reform left the benefits intact for these offshore insurers, and there has been a shift to this approach since 1986.)

While tax reform slowed down the boom in self insurance, it created an even bigger boom for private international bank owners willing to take over the insuring role. (Not surprisingly, 40 percent of the U.S. insurance market has now moved offshore.) Instead of setting up their own insurance subsidiaries, U.S. companies, trade groups, and professional associations can contract for coverage with private banks. The banks handle the insurance function in exactly the same fashion as the former captive operations, that is, with major benefits for both the insured parties and the bank owner.

The insured parties pay virtually the same premiums they paid to their own operations, receive the same level of coverage, and retain the advantage of less stringent regulation offshore. And, because they are buying their insurance from an independent entity, the premiums are deductible, and they have no tax liability on profits from investing the reserve pool (which can still be channeled back to them in the form of lower premiums).

The private international bank (which, as you will see in chapter 6, "Asset-Protection Benefits of a Private International Bank," gets its own liability protection by virtue of its offshore status) makes its money from administrative charges and fees it gets for managing the capital pool created by the premiums paid by the insured parties. In addition, once it has the structure in place, the bank can also offer management services to other cooperative insurance groups that want a base offshore; or, if the bank is well capitalized and has good management, it can even begin offering insurance coverage to other clients outside the original self-insurance group.

Insurance Savings

Just as the private international bank may offer insurance services at profit, an individual or a corporation that pays an excessive amount of annual insurance premiums can save money by using an international bank as its captive insurance company. In this situation, the bank acts as a financial cushion and receives insurance premiums from the parent owner. Any third parties who demand verification of insured status in a business venture may receive it from the insured company, which is bonded at a low cost.

The premiums the company pays may then be invested by the bank in portfolio ventures earning tax-free profits for the bank. According to tax regulations, the insurance premiums paid to the bank may be deducted if the bank also provides insurance for third parties. In other words, the bank that underwrites its parent must also underwrite unrelated companies or persons in order for the bank and corporation both to claim tax benefits of captive insurance and to benefit from low-cost insurance premiums.

LENDING SERVICES

The next profit-making area for a private international bank involves extending credit. There are five basic means of extending credit:

1. High-interest loans
2. Letters of credit, (i.e., financial instruments saying that if certain conditions are met, payment will be tendered)
3. Bank guarantees (i.e., financial instruments obligating an institution to act as guarantor on a loan)
4. Secured lending (or asset-based financing)
5. Back-to-back loans, in which a bank accepts a person's deposit and then relends him a certain amount for an onward transaction (the person's deposit is collateral for the loan)

Obviously, in any of these instances, if the bank issues credit, its assets must be adequate to support the loan.

High-Interest Loans

Nearly all private international banks take advantage of their ability to lend money. The most common type of lending a private international bank does involves venture capital: high-risk loans at high interest rates. Private international banks can make such loans—and charge such rates—because state usury laws generally do not apply.

As a result, your private international bank would be able to make high-interest loans to third parties—loans impossible to make without the bank's existence. The profit from such activity may be from 5 to 10 percentage points above that available to a conventional lender. (These high margins are essential to compensate the lender for the possibility of default by such high-risk borrowers.) Tax savings are associated with these lending services since profits from banking business as such are not taxed internationally.

Loan companies are particularly suited to take advantage of these lending benefits. By owning a private international bank, a U.S.-based loan company can make high-interest loans that would otherwise be illegal. And, again, interest income from such loans is tax free as long as it remains offshore.

Letters of Credit and Bank Guarantees

A bank's cash-flow position consists of more than cash. Assets and access to quickly liquid securities may be included in its capitalization. Provided the bank's capital structure in its entirety can support an extension of credit to a certain dollar amount, it may issue a letter of credit or financial guarantee.

Such instruments have a variety of applications that can benefit both the bank and its customers. For example, a bank guarantee may be used as a completion or performance bond for real-estate development or construction.

A letter of credit may also be used to purchase goods for import to the United States or to guarantee a loan from a third party. (See appendix B for sample.) For example, a private international bank could issue a letter of credit to a Hong Kong expatriate wishing to purchase electronics equipment. By using a letter of credit as a guarantee, his otherwise unsecured loan can become a secured loan.

A bank can profit from this situation, even if it has to borrow funds from another bank to back up the letter of credit, guarantee, or surety. The concept of bank-to-bank benefits enters at this point. A private international bank can borrow from another bank at an interbank lending rate much lower than the rate a regular borrower would be charged on a retail loan. Thus, the private bank has plenty of room to provide funds at a profitable margin while still giving the end borrower considerable cost savings over the interest rate on a normal loan. The private bank can profit further by charging a service fee or points for the issuance of such instruments as letters of credit and loan guarantees.

Margin Advantages

The government regulates credit in part through *margin requirements* for stock and bond purchases, futures transactions, and other investments. The margin is the percentage of the cost of a stock, bond, or future that a buyer must put up at the time of the purchase. The rest can be borrowed, with the financial instruments themselves serving as collateral.

A little-known area of investment opportunity for consumers involves margining securities through a private international bank. Ordinarily, an investor is extended a margin of 50 percent when purchasing listed stocks and 30 percent when buying bonds, pursuant to Regulation T of the Federal Reserve System. However, Regulation T does not apply to foreign banks.

Thus, an international bank is in a legal position to lend 100 percent on margin for the purchase of listed stocks, less any fee (points) collected for providing the service. The additional 50 percent that would ordinarily be required as margin for the purchase of the stock may be invested at the best possible return, thus reducing an investor's (or, more likely, the private international bank owner's) opportunity cost.

Secured Lending and Back-to-Back Loans

As mentioned in chapter 2, back-to-back loans are matching deposit arrangements that may be used to solve a financing or exchange-control problem, allowing diversified corporations to transfer profits from one business to another (usually from a high tax-base jurisdiction to one with a lower tax base). In an offshore environment, secured loans (also discussed in chapter 2) can be issued for high-risk projects at interest rates higher than those permitted by U.S. banking laws.

Cost Advantages of Lending

A major reason a private international bank profits by lending money is that it can borrow below prime rate. It may issue CDs or promissory notes denominated in a currency whose borrowing rate is lower than the U.S.-dollar prime lending rate. Suppose the borrowing rate for Swiss francs is 6.5 percent per annum but that the U.S. prime rate is 8.5 percent annually (as it was at the end of 1997). If an international bank were to borrow in Swiss francs at prime, it could convert the francs to U.S. dollars and loan the money to its current shareholders or customers at the higher U.S. rate.

To protect the bank's position in relation to the repayment of the loan in Swiss francs, it will likely have to purchase a futures contract or forward contract guaranteeing that the Swiss francs will be available at a specific and known price when the loan is due. This cost is known as a *hedge cost*, which ultimately increases the borrowing cost.

However, there is usually enough of a profit margin in the transaction that it normally works out lower than the cost of borrowing the equivalent amount of money in U.S. dollars. The bank is needed to issue the CD (the actual instrument of borrowing), save on the cost of exchange from Swiss francs to U.S. dollars, and maintain the futures contract in Swiss francs.

Investment Opportunities

Investing is an important profit area for any bank. And, by virtue of its foreign status, a private international bank can make many different types of investments prohibited for U.S. banks. Securities, commodities, and real estate as a principle investment are the most obvious examples.

The international bank structure is ideally suited to profiting from investment because, in accepting deposits, a bank is put in the position of raising investment capital. In effect, it is raising money under a new name. Thus, a private international bank is probably the best vehicle through which a domestic individual (or, indeed, a domestic bank) can raise capital in the international market at low cost and turn it to profit opportunity not normally available to U.S. investors.

The international bank structure is ideally suited to profiting from investment because, in accepting deposits, a bank is put in the position of raising investment capital. In effect, it is raising money under a new name. Thus, a private international bank is probably the best vehicle through which a domestic individual (or, indeed, a domestic bank) can raise capital in the international market at low cost and turn it to profit opportunity not normally available to U.S. investors.

Arbitrage

In the foreign money market or foreign-exchange market, quotations for the same currency vary from market to market during the day. Considering that an international bank will be permitted to purchase foreign exchange at a lower rate than ordinary customers, it may be able to earn significant profit by purchasing currency in one market and selling it at the same instant in another. When a bank trades to take advantage of the spread in price between markets, it is engaged in arbitrage.

Through its foreign-exchange trader in London, a private international bank may be able to purchase deutsche marks for its account in Frankfurt and sell these to another dealer for Italian lire. The bank may then find a broker who needs lire in another marketplace, such as Zurich, and receive deutsche marks as a result of the sale of the lire. When spreads and opportunity exist, it is possible to make cross-trades of this type in a matter of minutes. After deducting telephone and transfer expenses, the bank may then wind up with a virtually risk-free transaction that results in significant profit.

A more common type of arbitrage is known as *interest rate arbitrage*. This involves conversion of funds from one market to another for the purpose of obtaining a higher rate of interest than is available at the starting point. Such investments are usually short term. Alternatively, the movement of funds abroad through the exchange market makes those funds available at a lower interest rate than that obtainable in the foreign market.

Thus, arbitrage occurs where lower interest rates and foreign-exchange costs make it worthwhile. The private international bank is an ideal vehicle for interest-rate arbitrage for two reasons. First, such a bank has an opportunity to receive a more favorable brokerage rate for the purchase and sale of funds. Second, any profits earned internationally are considered to be related to the bank's business and are thus tax free.

In addition, the private international bank may be used to attract customers who wish this activity to be performed on their behalf. As individuals rather than banks, the persons availing themselves of income derived in this manner would not automatically be entitled to a tax benefit as would a bank, and a bank can pass that benefit on to its customers. The bank still earns income on a fee basis. Arising as it does from bona fide banking business, this fee income would be tax free.

Bank Float

Some people think profiting legally from a float is somehow unethical. In fact, float is foundational to the banking business. For example, Merrill Lynch routinely pays its New York customers with checks drawn on a bank in North Carolina, showing that the financial services giant fully understands the value of float. As a much bigger example, American Express Co., the world's largest issuer of traveler's checks, collects tens of millions in cash from people who buy the checks. It immediately invests this money into high-yield T-bills or similar money market instruments. The traveler's checks aren't cashed until days or even weeks later, perhaps in Japan, England or Italy, and don't make their way back to American Express for payment for a considerable length of time. American Express makes its money not only from the fee it charges a traveler but also from the interest it earns by investing the collected cash. This is the float—and it is not unethical to use it! It is simply good business practice.

Private international bank owners and customers alike can profit from the float—the owner by using the float as a marketing tool and the customer by using it to pay bills. If the holder of a private international bank account issues a check to a U.S. creditor, it must be sent by mail for collection because the international bank is not a member of the Federal Reserve Clearing System. This can take from a few days to several weeks. Meanwhile, as the check is finding its way back to the international bank, the depositor can earn a return on his money in his interest-bearing checking account.

WHOLESALE BANKING SERVICES

Although a large number of domestic banks failed during the 1980s and early 1990s, banking is still considered one of the most lucrative businesses in the United States—which is why more and more new domestic banks are formed each year. Unless they are grossly mismanaged, banks are able to make substantial profits by taking deposits and paying low rates of interest, meanwhile rolling the deposited funds into short-term, high-interest investments, such as T-bills, that bring a fast return and additional working capital. This growth of domestic banking is taking place despite a mass of federal and state regulations, a capitalization requirement of at least $2.5 million, a high reserve requirement, and restrictions on the types of allowable investments banks may make.

How much greater the opportunity is for a private international bank that enjoys minimal regulation, capitalization, and reserve requirements; far lower operating costs; and the power to function as a merchant bank. If such a bank can attract customers by means of well-targeted marketing, its margin of profit stands to be considerably greater than its domestic counterpart.

The Growth of Banking Services

The investing public today is looking increasingly for financial institutions capable of offering a wide range of services, such as investment in money market and mutual funds, brokerage services, personal loans, mortgages, credit cards, and international automatic teller (ATM) services. The more of these services a private international bank can offer, the more successful and profitable the bank will be overall.

To offer such services, of course, private international banks must purchase them from somewhere. In that sense, the independent bank is something like a retail merchant who buys financial services at wholesale prices and sells them at retail markup. The spread between the wholesale and retail prices is its gross profit. This is the principle of what, for convenience, we can call wholesale banking.

One aspect of wholesale banking involves tapping into a variety of money management services that private international banks can offer more cheaply and profitably than their domestic counterparts. A second aspect has to do with techno-electronic banking services—a relatively new and fast-evolving element of private international banking. In either case, the individual private bank is a retailer of services. Customers buy these services on the basis of the effectiveness with which the bank can market them.

Electronic Credit

International credit (and debit) cards and ATM services are a major part of wholesale banking. Visa charges banks a quarterly service fee of 0.30 percent of sales volume with a minimum of $1,500, which begins after a bank has been a Visa member for two full quarters. In addition, there is an interchange volume fee of 0.10 percent of volume. For the processing of applications, new Visa members must also pay an initial service fee of between $5,000 and $50,000, depending on the size of the bank's assets. Despite these and some other fees, for many private international banks, a credit-card business is well within financial reach.

In the area of electronic banking, private international banks can now tie into the major U.S. ATM networks. (Visa, Mastercard, and most other bank cards can be used to obtain cash from ATMs all over the world.) The opportunity for a private international bank lies in the fact that it can use this technology to attract customers from the United States as well as from other countries. By using ATM tie-ins, the international bank can collect customers' deposits, interest payments, and service fees from anywhere in the world.

Automated teller services are easily contracted. There is no shortage of ATM vendors. They'll be happy to install a machine in your living room, if you want—though obviously the economics are more feasible in a location with more foot traffic! But you don't need to maintain a full

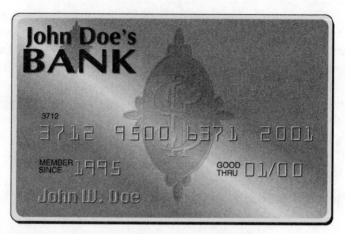

Figure 3.2.   Issue yourself your own credit card

banking establishment, simply an office. The independent vendor will order a phone line, then periodically fill the machine with currency and retrieve deposits.

Want Your Photo on a Credit Card?

You then issue your own custom offshore plastic—with the name of your bank, even your own portrait if you so choose!

In practice, most offshore credit cards are currently issued as "secured credit cards," meaning the holder has a line of credit generally around 50 percent of the amount on deposit in an interest-bearing savings account. In other words, such credit cards are really treated as debit cards. Or you may choose to issue "combination cards," which serve as cash, credit, and debit cards and may also be used for check guarantees.

Because electronic banking is so accessible, offshore banks are now competing vigorously with U.S. banks for

> **B**ecause electronic banking is so accessible, offshore banks are now competing vigorously with U.S. banks for the profitable credit- and debit-card business, with many competitive advantages clearly going to the offshore banks. The lack of privacy associated with American credit cards is a prime reason. . . . Offshore plastic, especially if issued by a jurisdiction with established banking secrecy laws, protects you from such privacy invasions.

the profitable credit- and debit-card business, with many competitive advantages clearly going to the offshore banks. The lack of privacy associated with American credit cards is a prime reason. Your offshore Visa or Mastercard provides detailed and intimate information on your daily habits—data that credit card companies analyze and resell to anyone who'll pay for it. Offshore plastic, especially if issued by a jurisdiction with established banking secrecy laws, protects you from such privacy invasions.

Because a private international bank collects fees for such electronic services, this obviously enlarges its profit potential enormously; and it also has important tax implications for the private international bank owner. Being linked to a worldwide ATM network demonstrates beyond a doubt that a private international bank is conducting banking business—and is doing so with customers who are "unrelated persons" within the meaning of IRS regulations. With such a body of proof on your side in any IRS query of your banking activities, you may be able to postpone indefinitely all taxes on earnings associated with your bank's operation.

WHOLESALE INVESTMENT SERVICES

The private international bank's role as a wholesaler of services can also be extended into the investment field. That's because banks are generally accorded special benefits by the investment industry—benefits that let a private international bank acquire the services of other banks or brokerage firms at reduced rates in order to resell them to its own customers at a profit. Thus, a private international bank, whether owned by an individual or a corporation, can usually save money on a variety of costs associated with doing business—most notably on investment commissions for such items as commodities, stocks, options, bonds, bullion, coins, currencies, and U.S. Treasury offerings.

Acting strictly as an agent, your private international bank can provide clients with brokerage services. The customer calls you with his order, which you place in the name of the bank with an established brokerage house. This way only you know the name of the customer. As far as the brokerage firm is concerned, your bank purchased the stock. Capital gains and dividends are automatically reported to the IRS, as brokerage firms are required to submit customer Social Security numbers and IRS Form 1099, which records a person's income from his trading account. But a bank has no Social Security number, nor are 1099 forms filed on them.

Thus, the individual investor gains privacy—and he is willing to pay your private international bank a commission to protect it. The commission is mostly profit since only a small record-keeping cost is incurred.

With relative ease, a private international bank can also offer such desirable investment services as money market funds and mutual funds, again making a handsome profit on the spread between the wholesale cost it pays for such services and the retail price at which it sells them to its customers.

INTERNATIONAL MONEY MARKET AND MUTUAL FUNDS

A private international bank can be more than just a retailer of other people's services. It can also generate substantial profits by providing those services itself, cutting out the middleman. Two of the most potentially profitable ventures involve mutual funds and money market funds.

The Money Market Mutual Fund

Mutual funds have been a popular form of investment for almost a century. Traditionally, mutual funds invested in stocks—and, of course, many still do. But, beginning in 1972, a new type of mutual fund emerged: the money market mutual fund. In 1979, these funds had assets of about $11 billion. By the end of 1994, more than $950 billion was on deposit in money market funds. Why? Quite simply, their benefits in times of both high- and low-interest rates are unbeatable.

Money market funds work on the premise that pooling resources is the best way small investors can maximize gains. Taking relatively small amounts of money from large numbers of investors, they hire the best investment advice available to look for the most desirable profit-making opportunities and invest accordingly. The result is a combination of yield, liquidity, and safety unmatched by more traditional investment programs.

The most important benefit to money market fund investors is yield. For relatively little money, the small saver can earn an interest rate about a half point below that received by investors with millions of dollars. The deposits placed with these funds earn interest from day of deposit to day of withdrawal and are not subject to a penalty for early withdrawal.

In addition, the funds are more liquid. Often, a checking account is included as part of the deal so the saver can withdraw money whenever he wants by simply writing a check for a specified minimum. Money market funds can afford to be liberal in terms of withdrawal rights because of the liquidity of their assets. Typically, their portfolio matures in less than thirty days. Conversely, banks and S&Ls have a high percentage of assets tied up in long-term investments such as twenty- and thirty-year mortgages—giving them far less flexibility than money market funds in setting interest rates paid to savers.

Safety is also a big marketing draw for these funds. Their favorite investment is commercial paper—unsecured, short-term promissory notes issued by such major corporations as IBM and AT&T. Certificates of deposit, both domestic and Eurodollar, are also popular. Domestic CDs, as a rule, require a $100,000 minimum deposit and are long-term. Their liquidity comes from secondary markets where they can be bought and sold. Eurodollar CDs are short term, sometimes held in overseas banks for periods as short as overnight. Other investments include U.S. Treasury obligations, government-agency issues, and repurchase agreements.

The safety record of money market mutual funds (to date, not a single money fund depositor has lost so much as a dollar) is important because it has been achieved despite the U.S. government's not providing deposit insurance. This has two important implications for private international banks. First, it means that an offshore bank can form an association with a money fund without subjecting itself to the onerous regulations and strict reserve requirements the government imposes on U.S. banks in exchange for providing deposit insurance through an agency such as the FDIC. This obviously gives the offshore bank a significant advantage over its domestic competition, which must not only deal with the added restrictions but also reduce deposit yields to offset the cost of the federal insurance.

Second, and more important, the safety record of the money funds can be used as a strong sales argument by private international bankers seeking new depositors. There is no shortage of Americans with ample reason to place a portion of their funds offshore. However, many are reluctant to do so for the simple reason that offshore banks do not have federal deposit insurance. By citing the outstanding safety record of the money funds, private bankers can make a strong case that deposit insurance is not needed in a true free-market investment environment, such as that enjoyed by offshore banks.

Why Deposit Insurance Is Not Needed

Most people fail to realize that protection of individual deposits is really the secondary purpose of federal deposit insurance. The primary reason for its existence is the prevention of a collapse of the American banking system, which is inherently unstable because it is based on debt rather than equity.

A bank fails for one simple reason: Depositors lose confidence in its solvency and stage a "run" on the bank, demanding a return of their deposits. This is usually prompted by a decline in the value of the bank's debt-based assets, as a result of either changing market conditions (e.g., the drop in real-estate values in oil-producing states like Texas during the mid-1980s) or a series of defaults by those who have borrowed from the bank.

However, money market funds are "runproof" because depositors actually own a share of the funds assets. Thus, any decline in the value of the fund's assets passes instantly to all fund shareholders, according to the proportion of the total shares they hold. Since shareholders cannot save what they have already lost, they have far less incentive to cash in their fund shares—unlike bank depositors, who can still claim the full value of their original deposit even when the bank no longer has enough assets to fulfill that claim.

Because of the nature of money fund investments, the odds against a substantial decline in the value of fund assets are high. As a result, most declines are small—causing only a small reduction in yield, not a major rush to liquidate fund shares. And, even if money fund shareholders do try to liquidate, they cannot threaten the solvency of the fund because they can withdraw only their pro rata share of whatever assets remain.

A private international bank can offer its depositors the same level of safety as the money market funds—even without any type of deposit insurance—by emulating the way the funds operate.

For those who question the validity of this approach in protecting the assets of depositors, there is a perfect example of the way it works inside the United States itself. IDS Certificate Co. of Minneapolis has been offering investors a CD—uninsured by the federal government or any other entity—since 1890. The CDs, actually called face amount certificates, have been highly successful for two reasons.

First, they have an extremely strong record of safety, having paid off even during the Great Depression. This safety is ensured by IDS's $2.35 billion portfolio of investment assets—98 percent of which is made up of short-term, investment-grade bonds—and its own equity reserve, which is maintained at a level sufficient to meet any unexpected influx of redemption requests.

Second, because IDS does not incur the administrative costs or pay the usual bank fees related to government deposit insurance, the certificates yield at least a quarter of a point more than bank CDs.

To more accurately define the resulting success of this "uninsured" deposit, IDS has had 1.2 million depositors over the years and sells almost $1 billion worth of the certificates annually.

Mutual Funds

People invest in mutual funds for the same reasons they invest in money market funds. There is strength in numbers. Top investment advice can be hired, increasing the potential for successful investment choices and thus increasing the potential yield. In addition, with many investors participating, a diversified portfolio can be created and a reserve established so that a degree of liquidity can be made available without forcing the sale of portions of the fund's stock portfolio.

Given the appeal of these two investment forms, it becomes clear that a private international bank offering its customers access to both money market funds and stock mutual funds has a strong competitive edge. More than ever, the public wants to deal with institutions that provide full service, and owners of private international banks can do this. The bank also gets added benefits since the offering of such popular services gives it a hedge against an unpredictable economy—it can attract investment funds no matter what the economic climate.

Making Funds Pay Off

As a bank owner, you can personally profit from money market and mutual funds by simply placing your investment funds with them and receiving their current yield. This is fine for a passive investor willing to take what the market offers. However, the aggressive entrepreneur can take it a step further, securing a piece of the action by actively promoting or running a money market or mutual fund.

You might think your small private international bank couldn't compete against Merrill Lynch or Citibank or the big fund families—but you'd be wrong. You can compete because you can offer advantages in the form of tax benefits and privacy that domestic firms cannot.

To be sure, there are considerable difficulties involved in setting up such funds. Legal requirements are far less stringent in international jurisdictions than they are domestically, but administering funds still requires expertise, careful planning, and attention to detail and procedure. Cost is also a major factor. Legal fees for setting up a money market fund domestically run about $250,000. In an international jurisdiction, these fees would be much less but could still run as high as $50,000.

The biggest obstacle, though, is the need for sophisticated financial expertise. Managing millions of dollars in investment monies calls for highly professional skills. Unless you are really knowledgeable about investments, you probably wouldn't choose to get involved at this level.

Acting as an Agent for Funds

Fortunately, there are easier—and still very profitable—ways of offering international money market and mutual funds. The private international bank owner can act as an agent for a fund, either indirectly or directly.

Being a direct agent for a fund is fairly simple. Your job is to seek new shareholders, which in effect makes you a marketing arm of the fund. You advertise, make contacts, and do whatever is necessary to attract clients. Administration and paperwork are kept to a minimum. Because you don't actually run the fund, you don't have the risks and costs of asset management.

Your income comes from the type of deal you arrange with the particular fund. Most likely, you'll work on straight commission. If you bring to the fund 250 shareholders, each of whom invests $20,000 (a typical money market fund investment), and you receive 2 percent as commission, you would gross $100,000.

Another possibility, applicable only to money market funds, has you functioning as an indirect agent, either in promoting an existing money market fund or as a marketer of your own bank's money market fund. In the latter instance, you wouldn't have to actually set up an independent money fund. You would create your own fund in name only. Though you solicit deposit funds in the name of your fund, most of the depositors' money is actually put into an established, well-known international fund.

You charge a small commission for doing so. Why would depositors be willing to pay you this commission? Because they more than make up for it in tax savings and convenience. In addition, you may decide to put only 80 percent of the money into a money market fund and deposit the remaining 20 percent in your own bank's CDs, thereby raising capital.

Obviously, you'll have to pay the market rate on this money. Say that the rate is 7 percent. You must invest this money so that it returns more than the 7 percent you're paying for it. This can be done by placing the money into cash management accounts that carry a higher risk factor than money market funds but that also pay more—let's say 8.5 percent. The difference is yours. Because of the risk involved, you wouldn't want to put more money into cash management accounts—which is a principle of your own international bank's financial management.

Tax Advantages

By keeping the money earned from international money market funds and mutual funds purchased through your bank offshore, the investor can avoid paying taxes on this income. Suppose an investor is in the 33 percent tax bracket

> The key is keeping international earnings offshore for as long as possible. This can be done by borrowing against the earnings. The investor takes out a loan against the amount he has earned from his overseas investment. This gives the desired liquidity and, if the money is used for business or investment, gives him a limited tax write-off for the interest he pays on the loan.

and is also subject to the 6 percent high-income surcharge, making his effective tax rate 39 percent. If he earned 10 percent on a domestic money market fund, or repatriated his international earnings, Uncle Sam would take 39 percent—meaning his true after-tax yield would be just 6.1 percent.

By keeping the interest payments offshore (which can be done only with an international money market fund), the investor keeps 100 percent of this money. Put another way, the investor would have to earn 16.4 percent from a domestic money market fund if he were to equal his return from an international fund paying 10 percent.

This is an exciting advantage, but people eventually will want to spend the interest payments and/or capital gains their international investments earn. This means bringing the money back to the United States, where they'll have to pay tax on it. However, the longer tax payments are deferred, the better. During the deferment period, the money that would have gone to Uncle Sam could be put to high-yield work.

The key is keeping international earnings offshore for as long as possible. This can be done by borrowing against the earnings. The investor takes out a loan against the amount he has earned from his overseas investment. This gives the desired liquidity and, if the money is used for business or investment, gives him a limited tax write-off for the interest he pays on the loan.

Domestic banks cannot equal this service because they cannot provide the tax and privacy advantages of a private international bank.

USING AN INTERNATIONAL BANK TO IMPROVE A FINANCIAL STATEMENT

Since international banks can conduct their affairs in a reasonably liberal and relaxed environment, they serve as useful vehicles to improve the financial reporting position of their parent shareholders as well as of their customers. Individuals and corporations may also find the use of an international bank effective in strengthening their financial statements or enhancing their credit. These techniques have been used by international bank-owning U.S. multinational corporations as well as by individual owners of private international banks.

Of course, any preparer of a financial statement will need to adhere to international accounting standards or rules established by the American Institute of Certified Public Accountants (AICPA). All methods suggested in this section are in conformity with AICPA guidelines and with generally accepted accounting principles.

Improving Cash Position

The private international bank offers the individual or company significant opportunity to improve its liquidity picture. The first item on a balance sheet in the assets column is "cash in the bank." Normally, this is also the strongest influencing factor for credit-granting purposes.

This figure would be footnoted to show that the individual or company involved in fact owns the bank. Thus, it would be regarded as a related-person transaction. However, this may be avoided by decontrolling the bank, either by owning less than 10 percent of its stock or having a third party own the bank.

Cash may be expressed in the cash column of the balance sheet in two ways: withdrawable cash (fully liquid) or CDs and time deposits. The latter implies restricted liquidity, but this is a fluid term these days. Assets now appearing on an individual or corporate balance sheet that can be converted to cash within several days may be placed into a private international bank and reported as cash in a current account with the bank.

The decision of what assets have immediate cash equivalency depends on the individual or firm involved. These assets may be cash-equivalent mutual funds, marketable securities, accounts receivable that are factorable within one or two days, liquid inventories, investment interest, insurance policies, or fixed assets that can be converted to cash on a moment's notice.

Assets on a balance sheet that take a longer time to convert to cash—such as real estate, equipment, automobiles, and furniture—can be re-expressed through a private international bank as a CD or a time deposit with the bank.

As an example, one of my clients owned some raw land. He wanted to get a loan based on that land, but domestic U.S. banks held that the land was unsuitable as collateral for a loan. To get around this, he "deposited" the land with his offshore bank for a set period of time. The bank carried the land on its books as a time deposit and was able to obtain a loan based on the increased value of its assets.

Improving Reported Debt

Debt on an individual or corporate balance sheet is one of the key factors in determining if a good loan can be made.

With the use of a private international bank, the debt picture may be converted to show a more sound financial picture. For example, short-term and contingent liabilities may be transferred to the bank's statement and re-expressed as long-term liabilities or notes payable to the bank.

Put another way, the company would refinance several short-term debts, consolidating them into one long-term obligation. For credit-granting purposes, a long-term obligation to a bank would appear more favorable on a balance sheet than short-term or contingent liabilities to several third parties.

What if the international bank does not have capital on hand to lend to the corporation for this purpose? It can use its bank status to seek favorable loan opportunities at a discounted rate, in turn discounting the consolidated loan to its parent.

Improving Assets in Net Worth

With the use of a private international bank and an unrelated person, the opportunity arises to show an increase in assets and/or net worth. This technique is often used by multinational corporations and commercial banks to enhance their balance sheets and to report higher earnings or more assets than would normally be reported.

The essential feature of this technique is that the transactions contemplated are conducted with unrelated persons. An unrelated person is a third party or corporation whose stock is less than 10 percent owned by those who stand to benefit. Unrelated persons may be a group of people, each of whom owns a portion of the stock of the third corporation.

The private international bank makes a loan to the unrelated person on a short-term basis. The bank reports on its statement the loan's interest as earned income. This income adds to the bank's net worth and earnings. The net worth and earnings then flow back to the parent shareholder, thus increasing the parent's net worth. The funds loaned to the unrelated person by the bank are then deposited back into the bank for a relatively long term at a low interest rate. The funds now back in the bank may be loaned out again to the unrelated person, thus showing more income, net worth, and earnings for the bank and thus increased net worth for the parent shareholder. Theoretically, an individual or a firm may legally increase its net worth by 50 to 100 percent, subject to certain limitations.

Critics of this technique claim that it is illegitimate because you are actually creating money! However, banks holding Eurodollars routinely recycle deposits among themselves to create a lot of money that is never available for use outside the banking system. And, under any concept of law where equal treatment of all is the foundation of the system, a bank is a bank is a bank.

AN OVERALL LOOK AT THE FINANCIAL PROSPECTS OF A PRIVATE INTERNATIONAL BANK

Now that you have seen the potential ways a private international bank can generate profits, here's an example of how such profits might fit into the total financial picture for an international bank. The tables on the following two pages provide a typical two-year operating statement for a Canadian-managed, Caribbean-based private international bank with an emphasis on financial services.

Note: The statements are for information and illustration purposes only and do not represent any actual bank in operation.

PRIVATE INTERNATIONAL BANK
(Financial Services Emphasis)
TWO-YEAR STATEMENT OF INCOME

FIRST-YEAR OPERATING RESULTS

INTEREST INCOME		
Loans Outstanding	$400,000	
Deposits and Other	$100,000	$500,000
INTEREST EXPENSE		
Deposits	$360,000	
Outstanding Debt	$ 7,500	$367,500
NET INTEREST INCOME	$132,500	
OTHER INCOME		
Commissions,Fees	$ 10,500	
Portfolio Management	$ 7,500	
Foreign Exchange	$ 10,000	
Escrow Fees	$ 1,000	$ 29,000
GROSS INCOME BEFORE EXPENSES	$161,500	
OPERATING EXPENSES		
Advertising and Promotion	$ 10,000	
Communications	$ 1,200	
Travel	$ 3,000	
Outside Services	$ 1,200	
First-Year Start-Up*	$ 45,000	
Bad Debt	$ 500	$ 60,900
NET INCOME BEFORE TAXES	$100,600	
INCOME TAX	$ 0	
TOTAL NET INCOME	$100,600	

*Amount may vary with changing market conditions.

PRIVATE INTERNATIONAL BANK
(Financial Services Emphasis)
TWO-YEAR STATEMENT OF INCOME

SECOND-YEAR OPERATING RESULTS

INTEREST INCOME		
Loans Outstanding	$800,000	
Deposits and Other	$200,000	$1,000,000
INTEREST EXPENSE		
Deposits	$720,000	
Outstanding Debt	$ 15,500	$ 735,500
NET INTEREST INCOME	$264,500	
OTHER INCOME		
Commissions, Fees	$ 21,000	
Portfolio Management	$ 15,000	
Foreign Exchange	$ 1,300	
Electronic Banking	$ 20,000	
Escrow Fees	$ 2,000	$ 59,300
GROSS INCOME		
BEFORE EXPENSES	$323,800	
OPERATING EXPENSES		
License Fee	$ 1,000	
Advertising and Promotion	$ 20,000	
Communications	$ 2,400	
Travel	$ 6,000	
Outside Services	$ 2,400	
Salaries	$ 1,700	
Bad Debt	$ 1,000	$ 34,500
NET INCOME BEFORE TAXES	$289,300	
INCOME TAX	$ 0	
TOTAL NET INCOME	$289,300	

A FINAL PROFIT BENEFIT: YOUR
BANK AS AN INVESTMENT

There is one final way in which a private international bank can generate profits for its owner, a method that many investors and businesspeople overlook. A private international bank can be extremely profitable as an investment in its own right. A successful private bank can be a valuable asset, and that value can increase considerably as a bank's success and reputation grow. This, then, raises two questions:

1. Just how much is your bank really worth?
2. Is it actually possible to accurately answer the first question?

In fact, the answer to the second question is probably no. While there are accepted methods for determining a bank's asset value, a tremendous number of intangibles make determining its actual resale value very difficult. The asset value of a private international bank is fairly easy to calculate: You simply measure the same factors that would be measured in considering the value of any bank, from giants like Bank of America to independents like the First State Bank of Anytown, U.S.A. Among considerations are physical facilities, number of clients, total deposits, loans outstanding, and liabilities—the kinds of things an accountant would look at in valuing most any business. However, to potential buyers, even a private bank that looks tiny by those tangible standards can be worth many times its owner's original cost because of the extreme importance of intangibles in determining value.

Perhaps the most important of these intangibles is reputation—so-called goodwill value—among depositors, borrowers, business associates, and even officials of the government in the bank's host nation. A small bank with a solid reputation and considerable goodwill can be worth several times more than a larger, less reputable bank.

Another significant factor is location. Small banks chartered and licensed in the more desirable offshore financial centers, such as tropical islands with a strong tourist appeal, are generally worth more than larger banks in less popular locales. There is similar value in market position. The biggest bank in one market will generally be worth more than the smallest bank in another market, even if the two are the same size in terms of assets.

Many other factors can also come into play in valuing a private bank, ranging from rate of growth and potential for future growth to management ability, marketing expertise, and investment performance. A fast-growing small bank will generally fetch a higher price than a larger, more stagnant institution—and a small bank that provides outstanding returns will have greater value than a larger one with a mediocre record.

The point is, your bank doesn't have to be a giant in the world of private international banking for it to be a valuable investment. In fact, not long ago a private international bank, originally purchased for just $30,000 and having only a few depositors, was sold to a New York investment banker for $100,000—a smart 233 percent return on the owner's money.

SUMMARY

The most common ways of profiting with a private international bank include the following:

- Accepting deposits and making loans
- Making sound investments with your bank's assets
- Engaging in currency-exchange activities
- Providing trust and cash management services
- Issuing various types of CDs to tap into the Eurodollar and flight-capital markets

- Providing offshore insurance services
- Providing letters of credit and bank guarantees
- Providing brokerage services
- Engaging in arbitrage activities involving currencies, Treasury securities, or other investment vehicles
- Marketing wholesale banking services, such as access to ATM networks and credit-card systems
- Installing ATMs or getting your own ATM cards to create your own identity
- Forming and operating your bank's own money market or regular mutual fund—or acting as an agent for existing international funds

There are many other ways a private international bank can be used in a profitable manner, depending on your professional or business abilities, personal needs, and willingness to expand your investment horizons. A quality bank management service will be able to help you customize your bank's activities to produce the maximum profit.

Whatever methods you choose as the focus of business for your bank, legally reducing or avoiding the tax burden on your business, investment, or private banking activities will be a major concern (and a major source of personal profits).

However, to claim the tax-related benefits of private international banking, you must first shield them from unwarranted scrutiny by creditors, competitors, and government agencies. The techniques for accomplishing this are discussed in the next chapter.

CHAPTER 4

PRIVACY BENEFITS OF A
PRIVATE INTERNATIONAL BANK

For most investors, privacy is of primary importance. In fact, it ranks right after profit as the concern that brings more prospective clients to my office. They feel—and rightly so—that it is an inherent right of each person to keep his or her finances confidential. The stories they tell me—of corporate and governmental intrusion—grow more horrific each year. I only wish they were fiction, but they are inescapable fact. In today's America, privacy has become virtually nonexistent.

Under U.S. law, creditors, litigants, private detectives, and forensic accountants are given the right to find out how much money a person has in the bank. Acting under the noble banners of "crime prevention" and "national security," the U.S. government has steadily moved to break down the walls of personal privacy. What the government seemingly fails to realize is that there are dozens of valid reasons for maintaining financial privacy. The desire to protect that privacy does not mean that an individual is a criminal.

In fact, the vast majority of the reasons for wanting financial privacy—yes, even from the government—are perfectly legitimate. In his book the *Complete Guide to Financial Privacy*, noted privacy advocate Mark Skousen identifies six specific reasons for maintaining a low financial profile:

1. Discrimination.   There are many types of discrimination a person can fall victim to—racial, religious, and political, to name three. Regardless of the type, if a government body can control or simply monitor the financial activities of the group being persecuted, it becomes almost impossible to fight the discrimination—or to flee, if that becomes the last resort. For example, without financial reserves outside Germany, even fewer Jews would have been able to escape Hitler's tyranny leading up to World War II.

2. Excessive government.   If a government knows every detail of its citizens' lives, then government "by the people and for the people" becomes an empty slogan. By restricting currency movements, prohibiting ownership of currency substitutes (such as gold or gems), and imposing confiscatory taxes, a government can control travel, business, investment, and wealth accumulation. In so doing, it can stifle opposition and prevent attempts at reform.

3. Threats to your reputation.   Nothing can damage your business or career more quickly than questions regarding your ability to handle money—which could arise if a bad investment, past business failure, or earlier bankruptcy were public knowledge. In addition, your investments can lead to false assumptions about your motives. For example, innocently buying stock in a company that did business in South Africa could have badly damaged your image in the late 1980s. Finally, if your financial activities are exposed, you are open to resentment by people doing worse than you—and scorn by those doing better.

4. Divorce, family disputes, and lawsuits.   These are the most common areas where the need for financial privacy arises. The exposure to damage if your enemies, competitors, creditors, or antagonistic family members know your personal assets is obvious. And this is the area where private international bank ownership can offer the most protection. (For a detailed discussion, see chapter 6, "Asset-Protection Benefits of a Private International Bank.")

5. Exposure to crime.   The more apparent your financial well-being, the more likely you are to be a target of robbers and burglars—as well as more sophisticated criminals who view you as a candidate for fraud, extortion, or even kidnapping.

6. "Legal fraud."   Nothing can expose you to high-pressure sales, promoters of shady investment deals, and plain old price rip-offs faster than public knowledge that you are financially well off.

Clearly, then, there are many legitimate reasons for wanting to maintain financial privacy. Yet the government continues to ignore these concerns, exposing the financial affairs of millions of honest citizens under the cover of tracking and catching a few thousand drug dealers, illegal stock traders, and organized crime figures. And the government is not alone in its "snoopervision." With minimal effort, a private investigator can uncover a frighteningly comprehensive picture of one's entire personal and financial situation and possibly expose those details in an embarrassing lawsuit.

In fact, there is one U.S. company—International Intelligence Network Corp.—whose sole business is monitoring personal data. This outfit, which has done work for many large companies and financial institutions, police departments, and state and federal taxing agencies—conducts open seminars on Public Information and Records Tracking

(PIRT). These seminars demonstrate how to obtain detailed information on anyone using nothing but public records. Here are some of the data that International Intelligence Network teaches its seminar attendees to uncover:

Information Regarding an Individual That May Be Obtained from a Complete Public Records Search

Full name, any aliases, AKA (also-known-as) records, and DBA (doing-business-as) statements

Date and place of birth, parents' names, and citizenship

Residence address and all phone numbers

Business address and all phone numbers

Additional present or past addresses

Marital status, date and place of marriage, spouse's maiden name, and names of spouse's parents

Children's names, addresses, and occupations

Occupation, length of time at present occupation, prior occupations, and spouse's occupation

Educational background and memberships in educational and civic associations

Complete military service record

Social Security number and date and state of issue

Present and past banks, S&Ls, CDs, and the names of officers at those financial institutions

Trust arrangements, including beneficiary, donor, and trustees

Inheritances, inventories of estates, probate, or wills

Records of asset sales

Records of loans outstanding and collateral offered, including mortgages and loans for automobiles, boats, and any other assets purchased by financing

Mortgages held and receivables from those mortgages

Personal or business assets owned, including real estate, equipment, automobiles, airplanes, and boats, and valuation of those assets for property taxes

Businesses or corporations owned, in whole or in part, including any DBAs; present corporate address; charter number; charter date and standing; names of all incorporators, officers, and directors; corporate capitalization; and names and locations of any subsidiaries or parent companies

Names of any registered agents or addresses used either personally or professionally

Limited partnership associations

Tax liens, date, and type of tax

Securities exchange 10-K filings and bank stocks owned

Names of current or past attorneys and the date, case, case number, court, and location where they served as a representative

Number and nature of legal cases in which person was a defendant and a brief of those cases

Number and nature of legal cases in which person was a plaintiff and a brief of those cases

Damages due from or owed as a result of litigation

Names of current or past accountants

Liquor or other state licenses owned

Records of bankruptcies

Criminal records or notes on other court appearances

Lists of known associates, mentions in newspapers, and other media-related information

If that list isn't sufficiently chilling, consider this: With computerized databases and a global information-service economy, all financial transactions are coming under even more careful scrutiny. Electronic communication systems can instantaneously interact, call up, compare, and

> **W**ith computerized databases and a global information-service economy, all financial transactions are coming under even more careful scrutiny. Electronic communication systems can instantaneously interact, call up, compare, and exchange information about you or me in the blink of an eye. Every time you cash a check, apply for credit, purchase an insurance policy, seek employment, or attempt to enter a facility with controlled access, you are asked to provide information regarding your personal money matters.

exchange information about you or me in the blink of an eye. Every time you cash a check, apply for credit, purchase an insurance policy, seek employment, or attempt to enter a facility with controlled access, you are asked to provide information regarding your personal money matters.

Annual income-tax filings and other financial reporting requirements collect additional data, making you that much more susceptible to intrusive probes by outside sources.

Unfortunately, such intrusive examples abound. The surveillance society is spreading both in the government and in corporate America. Here are a few more ways in which your privacy is under attack:

- In 1990, the U.S. Treasury Department created the Financial Crimes Enforcement Network (FinCEN). Acting with the IRS' Computing Center in Detroit and the five federal bank regulatory agencies, the FinCEN has established a suspicious-activity reporting system, a computerized data bank available to all major law enforcement agencies. Then Treasury decided to spread its net wider, keeping, in computer files, the names and addresses of all Americans with foreign bank accounts.

- New technologies allow private investigators and government agencies to eavesdrop on telephone lines without detection.

- In 1997, a team of IRS internal auditors, operating a sting, found that its employees browsed through taxpayer records, looking into the incomes of celebrities, relatives, and former spouses. Another sting discovered that income data on other taxpayers could be easily obtained over the phone—using only a name, an address, and a Social Security number. The auditors successfully obtained confidential tax information in 96 out of 109 telephone calls, including those in which investigators posed as other taxpayers.

- In January 1998, the IRS admitted it ranked employees on their aggressiveness in collecting delinquent taxes and conducting seizures of property, practices that violate laws intended to protect Americans from overzealous tax enforcement.

- Banks in the United States are planning to issue so-called smart cards, with microchips capable of storing a huge amount of personal data. The idea is for such "know-it-all" cards eventually to become indispensable, almost a de facto identity card—at least until better technology comes along. "In 15 years, it may not be a card at all," says Carl F. Pascarella, president of Visa USA. "It could be your palm."

- The government is introducing new U.S. currency featuring magnetic threads within the paper so the movement of money can be more closely monitored.

- The Passport Office has already begun issuing a machine-readable passport that can be used to monitor airline reservations, financial transactions, and all movements by an individual into and out of the country. (This obviously includes travel to and from offshore havens.)

* Big Brother is definitely watching the borders. The Anti-Crime Act of 1986 allows U.S. customs agents to search through baggage and mail without a warrant or permission. And this authority applies to all *departing* as well as *returning* travelers. So, at their discretion, airport customs officials may now investigate what you take out of this country as well as what you bring back into it.

* The Supreme Court has ruled that evidence obtained illegally by the IRS can be used to convict a taxpayer—a decision that will encourage future covert action and government misconduct against "suspected citizens."

* Your medical records are open to inspection. While most doctors, on purely ethical grounds, try to see that your records are kept private, there's no guarantee. Insurance companies can subpoena your records for lawsuits or simply have them pulled from a computer data bank, where most medical files are stored these days. Most people don't realize it, but medical confidentiality does not actually exist by law—it's really just a matter of tradition. If the doctor is willing or is subjected to pressure, he or she can legally give your records to anyone—lawyers, reporters, law officers, investigators—even your friends.

* The largest data-collection firm, TRW, maintains files on some 120 million Americans, with emphasis on their credit histories. Lenders nationwide can request from TRW, or from any of several competitors, detailed information about your income, debts, employment history, marital status, tax liens, judgments, arrests, and convictions. There are about two thousand separate credit bureaus in the United States, and they *all* harbor data that could dam-age you.

* Equifax Services of Atlanta sells over twenty million reports each year on individual health habits and lifestyles

to prospective employers and insurers. The results can be ruinous, especially when the information is completely false. For example, a California woman was unable to buy health insurance because an emergency-room physician treating her after a diabetic attack wrongly diagnosed her as being an alcoholic. And computerized misinformation, whether through malice or incompetence, is rampant. An estimated half of all FBI records are inaccurate or incomplete. State criminal records are said to be anywhere between 12 and 49 percent accurate, and only 13 percent of all federal agencies bother to audit their own systems for accuracy.

- Chicago-based Docket-Search Network sells a service called "Physician's Alert," providing information to doctors on patients who have filed civil suits.

- Moscom, the world's leading supplier of call-accounting computer systems, lets employers track all their workers' on-the-job phone calls—who they call and how long they talk.

- Marc Rotenberg, director of the Electronic Privacy Information Center in Washington, D.C., warns about hightech organizational monitoring efforts. "The more sophisticated the organization, the more likely it will want to do things like keep tabs on electronic mail and computer systems usage." For example, how much time is that auditor spending on those electronic spreadsheets? Why does this senior manager send out proportionately more e-mail but get so little in reply? Yesterday we couldn't answer those questions cheaply. Today we can. Tomorrow we can monitor even more for less.

- There are about eighty-five federal databases on 114 million people. A network of fifteen federal regulatory and enforcement agencies routinely mixes and matches data. The Department of Education uses it to locate wage earners who have defaulted on student loans. By comparing its lists with state driver's license records, the Selective

Service can ferret out the names of young men who have failed to register for the draft. And the IRS flags taxpayers who underreport by matching tax returns with information from employers, stockbrokers, mutual funds, and insurers of stocks and bonds.

- Using its debtor master file, the IRS routinely withholds tax refunds to people who owe money to the Department of Education, the Department of Housing and Urban Development, the Veterans Administration, and the Small Business Administration.

- The FBI routinely reviews subjects' criminal, financial, medical, and motor vehicle histories. During the Clinton White House file scandal, one person under security review had to sign a waiver so the FBI could interview her therapist. The IRS denies that it releases any individual's returns to the FBI. (If so, the FBI could get most of what it wants from the subject's bank manager.)

- The Supreme Court has ruled that police and other government authorities can paw through your garbage in search of incriminating evidence. A warrant isn't even required once you have placed the trash at curbside for collection.

The logical solution to all this surveillance, of course, is to keep silent about all personal and financial affairs, minimizing the amount of information that gets created about you. This makes eminent sense, since experts say that we ourselves provide government and private industry most of the data they maintain on us. In fact, one study concludes that more than 72 percent of the time, investigators obtain their information from those they are monitoring.

But clamming up is far easier said than done, especially when the questions come from a government that has authority over much of your life. As the federal bureaucracy tightens its grip on the movement of money—within the country and outside it—your personal privacy withers.

PRIVACY AND BIG GOVERNMENT

It was not always so difficult to maintain privacy—financial or otherwise. Our right to conduct personal affairs without outside intrusion was originally secured by the Bill of Rights. The First Amendment's guarantee of freedom of speech, press, assembly, and right of petition for redress of grievances would seem to ensure free communication between investors and their financial advisers. Whether the communication is conducted by mail, over the telephone, or through individual intermediaries, U.S. citizens should be free to exchange information regarding distribution and diversification of their assets.

And if the federal government decides to check your mail or monitor your calls to collect information on your financial transactions, your First Amendment rights are in all probability being violated.

Yet the SEC has restricted financial advice and communication for more than fifty years. The Investment Advisors Act of 1933 requires all financial advisers and investment newsletters to be registered with the SEC (though the courts eased that restriction somewhat with the *Lowe* decision of

It was not always so difficult to maintain privacy—financial or otherwise. Our right to conduct personal affairs without outside intrusion was originally secured by the Bill of Rights. The First Amendment's guarantee of freedom of speech, press, assembly, and right of petition for redress of grievances would seem to ensure free communication between investors and their financial advisers.

1987, which exempts newsletters not actually giving specific one-on-one advice). All investors and their advisers must utilize certain accounting procedures. If business transactions are conducted in any other way, both individuals may be found in violation of the law.

The act also gives the SEC authority to enter an adviser's or publisher's office without warning for the sole purpose of inspecting accounts and mailing lists. It requires investment advisers to forewarn all clients that the purchase of unregistered foreign stocks carries certain legal risk. All of this violates the spirit of the First Amendment because it limits free communication. It also violates the Fourth Amendment, which protects against unreasonable searches and seizures without probable cause.

Fourth Amendment Rights Disappear at Domestic Banks

In 1970, Congress passed the Bank Secrecy Act (Public Law 91-508), requiring all domestic banks to maintain duplicate records of their transactions. Specifically, the law actually authorizes an invasion of your privacy by requiring banks to make "a microfilm or other reproduction of each check, draft or similar instrument drawn upon it and presented to it for payment" and "a record of each check, draft, or similar instrument received by it for deposit or collection, together with an identification of the party for whose account it is to be deposited or collected."

Banks were also instructed to keep records of every check written over $100, as well as cash transactions (deposits and withdrawals) over $10,000. And they must record all credit transactions over $5,000. As a further encroachment, all new accounts require a Social Security number or taxpayer ID number. Should an individual fail to comply within forty-five days, his or her name, address, and account numbers are put on a list for inspection by the IRS.

The legislative premise of such outrageous intrusions on banking privacy has been that "an effective fight on crime depends, in large measure, on the maintenance of adequate and appropriate records by financial institutions."

Do I turn a blind eye on financial crime? Absolutely not. I don't condone illegality of any kind. Criminals, white-collar and otherwise, should be tracked down and prosecuted. Those who evade lawful U.S. taxes need to be identified by the IRS. But neither do I condone government agencies trampling on the freedoms of innocent citizens in their zeal. And, make no mistake, we end up being the real targets of this bureaucratic overkill, not the few career criminals, who are often skillful at circumventing legal mandates. For every outlaw put temporarily out of commission, millions of law-abiding Americans have been stripped of their financial privacy.

Predictably, the Bank Secrecy Act unleashed a host of government fishing expeditions, and the courts upheld this intrusion into financial privacy. In *United States v. Miller*, the Supreme Court ruled that bank customers whose records are sought by the government for whatever reason have no right to ensure that access is controlled by an "existing legal process."

This literally opened America's banks to any government agency able to get a subpoena or court order. And, based on the precedent involving the government, the courts subsequently granted similar rights to private parties involved in any kind of legal case. Obviously, with this kind of leeway, there are bound to be tremendous and costly abuses. I know of one legal case that was lost because of supposedly secure financial information released after a process-server presented a subpoena to a bank's receptionist, who processed the request without even checking for clearance from an appropriate bank officer.

Even when there is no direct abuse, there is danger to people who may even be uninvolved in a case. A bank in Los Angeles was forced to turn over one depositor's financial records merely because he had dated a woman involved in a divorce case. The disgruntled husband felt the man might be assisting in his estranged wife's support or helping her conceal assets that would impact his alimony payments and the property settlement, so he asked for the records—and the court granted his request!

To be fair, Congress attempted to redress some of these excesses, but its remedy was far from perfect. The Tax Reform Act of 1976 (TEFRA) included a provision allowing onshore bank customers to challenge the IRS in the event the agency decided to seize bank records. However, the Congress left one gaping loophole in the act. It gave the IRS an exemption from the restriction when the person being investigated was "suspected of a crime" but offered no clear definition of what "suspected of a crime" really means, leaving that determination up to the IRS.

In addition, it imposed no restrictions on enforcement agencies other than the IRS. The upshot is that you have no legal recourse if a grand jury, the FBI, or the local police seizes your records. Thus, the law has been a dismal failure with respect to restoring Fourth Amendment rights.

Fifth Amendment Rights Also Threatened

Financial privacy is also a fundamental issue in the Fifth Amendment, which states that no citizen "shall be compelled in any criminal case to be witness against himself, nor be deprived of life, liberty or property, without due process of law." Protection from self-incrimination is a relevant point in any tax-evasion case. But it has a bearing in terms of alleged fraud and other lawsuits.

There is no question that release of a person's private financial records and related papers to the opposition in a legal case can be highly incriminating. While the courts have recognized this, they have unfortunately adopted a very narrow definition of "private papers" as related to financial records. Recent rulings have held that the only records protected are those held by the individual. Financial papers held by a domestic bank or the individual's attorney, accountant, or any other third party are unprotected—meaning they can legally be seized for use in a court case against the individual.

What's worse, a person can be convicted on the basis of records illegally obtained. During the Watergate scandal, the IRS, CIA, and FBI were shown to have been routinely opening the mail of selected persons, sometimes in pursuit of those on an "enemies list." In one case, IRS Project Haven, the tax men actually stole documents used in prosecutions for tax evasion. Opening of mail has supposedly stopped, but the courts have continued to rule that evidence illegally obtained by the IRS is admissible.

Note: One solution, for those deeply concerned about the tampering of mail to or from an international banking center, might be to use a mailing service located, for example, in Canada. A mail-forwarding service can place all materials in a plain envelope, reducing the risk of undue attention from investigative agencies. Such a service can also forward your internationally bound mail to your resident agents or others.

Loss of Privacy by Error

There have been a few victories for personal privacy. In 1978, the Financial Privacy Act essentially overruled the *Miller* decision. Today, the federal government must notify you before—and give you the opportunity to challenge—any record search. Banks, savings and loan associations, and credit-card companies all fall under the wording of the act.

In addition, numerous members of Congress, led by Sen. David Pryor of Arkansas, passed the so-called Taxpayer's Bill of Rights, which, among other things, reverses the burden of proof in tax-evasion cases from the taxpayer to the IRS. Then, in the fall of 1997, with the spectacular public response to the Senate Finance Committee's hearings on IRS abuses, President Clinton dropped his opposition to Republican efforts to restructure the IRS, and the House voted to place the IRS under an independent oversight board.

Still, the damage has largely already been done. One of the biggest privacy problems today is that, with so much confusion in the domestic banking industry relating to disclosure rules and government rights of access, your financial records could be released by mistake—sometimes with disastrous results. A few more horror stories will graphically illustrate the point:

- The IRS sent a written request for a bank customer's financial records to a midwestern bank. The bank officer who received the request, assuming the government was acting within its rights, forwarded the records without asking the customer's permission or demanding a subpoena from the IRS. The customer was subsequently audited and held liable for penalties on the basis of information improperly obtained from his own bank records.

- A California bank received two information requests on the same client during the same week—one from a state agency, which requires no disclosure to the customer, and one from the SEC, which requires a subpoena. The requests were mixed up by bank personnel, and the client's financial records were improperly released to the SEC.

- A New York bank received a query from the Social Security Administration about the account of a widow. The widow had no account, but the bank did hold the account of a trust that listed the widow as beneficiary. Assuming the requirements for a trust were the same as for an individual, the records were supplied, and the widow's Social Security benefits were subsequently reduced.

All these cases involve clear violations of the Right to Financial Privacy Act of 1978, yet they happened. And, unfortunately, the only smart-money bet is that they will keep on happening.

THE PRIVACY ALTERNATIVE

The evidence is overwhelming: Our most basic rights to privacy are being systematically violated by a government originally designed to protect its citizens from undue intrusion. Seen in this light, the United States is far too risky an environment for investors concerned with financial privacy. Why keep assets within the country, knowing that your banking transactions are monitored by the federal government, when you can maintain those holdings, in privacy, internationally?

Private international banks have thus become an important tool in preserving and protecting investor privacy. Aware of this problem—and convinced of the validity of

Private international banks have thus become an important tool in preserving and protecting investor privacy. Aware of this problem—and convinced of the validity of the theory that confidentiality breeds confidence—international financial-center governments continue on a competitive basis to strengthen their privacy laws in order to accord U.S. investors and business operators an impenetrable sanctuary.

the theory that confidentiality breeds confidence—international financial-center governments continue on a competitive basis to strengthen their privacy laws in order to accord U.S. investors and business operators an impenetrable sanctuary.

USING OFFSHORE BANKS CAN ENHANCE YOUR PRIVACY

By establishing your own private bank, or using a private bank in an offshore jurisdiction not partners with the United States in an information-sharing system, you can dramatically enhance your privacy. Specifically, the private international bank represents one of the best vehicles to achieve total financial privacy. In fact, keeping your financial affairs completely confidential is possible *only* when that wealth is offshore. This is because individuals are not readily associated with bank ownership.

For example, assets placed into a private international bank are camouflaged, for the most part, by the activities of other commercial banks and thus do not attract unnecessary attention on accounting ledgers. A remittance to a private international bank in the form of an interest payment may be journaled as a payment to AB Bank Ltd. (perhaps a payment ordinarily made to a U.S. bank). If the interest payment is made to a foreign corporation that is not a bank, its appearance is more prone to challenge upon audit. Likewise, loans or loan proceeds received from a bank attract less attention than loans received from an ordinary corporation.

Funds kept in a private international bank may be entered on a ledger or balance sheet as "cash in bank." More revealing would be a notation such as "a deposit in AB Corporation." This is a veritable red flag for an IRS auditor or agent eager to advance within the bureaucratic hierarchy.

INTERNATIONAL BANKING: PRIVACY INSURANCE

The unique status of banks offers an added benefit to the investor or businessperson wishing to move or invest capital internationally. International officials have long been aware that investors desire banking privacy. To this end, most have competitively strengthened their regional secrecy laws to accord international customers an impenetrable financial sanctuary.

Of course, the federal government would like to curtail the international banking boom. After all, the money this country loses every year to foreign centers could help reduce our staggering national debt (though, of course, Congress would end up spending every confiscated penny and more). One of Uncle Sam's weapons against offshore flight is intimidation-by-treaty. With respect to financial privacy, it should be noted, however, that tax treaties do not necessarily constitute information-sharing treaties or arrangements, though the IRS has threatened to unilaterally break such treaties where secrecy laws may prevent their gaining access to private international bank records.

During the 1980s, the Reagan Administration sought to coerce certain international jurisdictions by reminding them that the U.S. government can, at any time, discontinue financial aid by terminating its Caribbean Basin Initiative, a regional economic development plan. The Bahamas, the Cayman Islands, Panama, and the Netherlands Antilles were threatened with the loss of annual subsidies for failing to cooperate with U.S. tax investigations. Government officials also launched a virtual worldwide campaign to entice— or bully—governments in other areas of the globe to sign tax treaties or information-sharing agreements with the United States.

In 1996, twenty-one members of the Organization of American States, meeting in Caracas, Venezuela, signed the U.S.-drafted Inter-American Convention Against Corruption, which made sweeping changes in national laws and ethics, limited bank secrecy, promoted openness of government operations, and provided for the extradition of corrupt officials.

Such proposals continue to be brought up from time to time and certainly bear watching. However, international business is so important to many of the Caribbean and Pacific-Asian countries affected that most have been reluctant to go along with the United States—some even considering the rejection of U.S. foreign aid in order to maintain bank secrecy and national sovereignty.

TAX TREATIES AND SECRECY LAWS

Businessmen and investors whose financial affairs are effectively and legally connected to a jurisdiction with a secrecy law can claim secrecy benefits. In most areas, these laws apply to banks operating domestically. Therefore, the best way to claim secrecy is to do business as a bank and state that all transactions are the bank's.

Bank secrecy could protect you from prying credit bureaus, unfair credit-card companies, prospective (and prospecting) heirs, the financial pain of divorce, or a government "fishing" expedition. Some privacy-conscious people sell property to the bank, then lease it back. Because the bank, not the person, holds title to the property, it cannot be attached in a lawsuit with the person. Most good international secrecy laws provide protection for the following:

- Books and records held by professionals
- Books and records held by banks
- Bank records and transactions
- Records held outside the jurisdiction
- Records of communications held by common carriers

In any case, tax treaties are simply an agreement between countries for the fairness and equalization of taxes in various matters. National economies, not matters of national sovereignty, are the issue.

Put another way, most international banking centers in the Caribbean or the Pacific-Asian region would take the position that they may order their internal financial affairs as they like. They need not obey a demand by the tax collector from another country to disclose the financial affairs of those operating in their jurisdiction.

For example, the United States has a tax treaty with the United Kingdom, but that does not prevent the British colonies from assuming their roles as some of the world's most advantageous tax havens. The reason is that the treaty is very specific with regard to the type of cooperation required in financial matters. Only when there is proof of criminal intent by a banking customer does the treaty require sharing of financial information—and the treaty spends four full pages carefully defining exactly what constitutes "criminal intent." It even goes so far as to provide for cooperation only in cases of "willful" criminal actions and uses four paragraphs to clarify what kind of "willful" activities fall under the treaty.

As a result, the British colonies can offer maximum financial secrecy to almost anyone who has not yet been at least indicted for an unlawful offense in the United States. In this way political principle serves the interests of financial creativity—and this is the power of private international banking.

The secrecy laws in international banking centers provide a guarantee of privacy and confidentiality for foreign bank owners and their clients, which affects directors, agents, employees, and customers. Some of the better havens even provide fines and jail sentences for anyone breaching the bank secrecy laws.

And, as pressure from the United States increases, many international centers are growing more adept at circumventing complex red tape and international regulation. Obviously, not every international center offers such extreme financial privacy since countries vary a great deal in their commitment to confidentiality. But they are all acutely aware that they will successfully attract and maintain foreign capital only if they offer maximum banking secrecy.

For example, Switzerland was once considered the ultimate bastion of banking privacy. As a result, it was the world's most powerful international money center. But the Swiss ethic and psychology shifted. Since 1982, the decay of the Swiss banking secrecy provisions has been reported on often in the world press. Much of the damaging information in the Iran-Contra arms-for-hostages scandal during the Reagan Administration was uncovered, thanks to the ability of the United States to get Swiss banking records. And a whole string of deposed Third Word rulers—from Panamanian strongman Gen. Manuel A. Noriega and Philippines President Ferdinand Marcos and Haitian dictator Jean Claude "Baby Doc" Duvalier—discovered to their dismay that the once-vaunted Swiss secrecy laws no longer provide much protection. (Duvalier also had millions tucked away in banks in New York, London, Luxembourg, Paris, and Geneva.)

This trend toward cooperation between the Swiss and U.S. governments has prompted a number of investors and businessmen to seek alternatives to Swiss banking. Switzerland's high profile in the international banking community and its increasing compliance with U.S. regulatory authorities on insider trading, tax evasion, and other criminal matters (e.g., money laundering and the disposition of drug-trafficking profits) have made most privacy-conscious investors concerned about information-sharing arrangements or agreements with the United States.

And, unfortunately, Switzerland is not alone. The Cayman Islands have gotten a tremendous amount of negative publicity about illegal activities of persons using banking facilities there. As a result, the Caymans have also become much more cooperative with U.S. authorities. And

> The lesson to be learned is that it can be dangerous to trust completely in any location's secrecy laws—no matter how airtight they appear. The simple truth is that laws change; they get overturned or overthrown. For this reason, investors seeking privacy protection should constantly monitor legal developments here and abroad.

many Caribbean banks now require from new customers a passport or other photo ID, Social Security or driver's license number, and even a reference letter from a previous bank.

The lesson to be learned is that it can be dangerous to trust completely in any location's secrecy laws—no matter how airtight they appear. The simple truth is that laws change; they get overturned or overthrown. For this reason, investors seeking privacy protection should constantly monitor legal developments here and abroad. Make a habit of comparing various international jurisdictions (an analysis of some leading centers is featured in chapter 9). Then move to transfer your assets before someone else moves to seize them.

OTHER PRIVACY BENEFITS GAINED THROUGH PRIVATE INTERNATIONAL BANKS

Enforcement agencies in the United States are intent on collecting information about citizens' international business dealings. But to concentrate only on the ways in which a private international bank cloaks assets from the federal government is to ignore its many other privacy benefits. For American businessmen in particular, private international banking offers myriad privacy protections.

Aggressive Competition

One of the most important privacy benefits obtained from private international banking is practical protection from overly aggressive competitors. Suppose you become involved in a business lawsuit. If you bank within the United States, a court may give your opponent legal access to your financial records, and your position may be seriously jeopardized. If your records are kept in a private international bank, they are impervious to court orders.

Private international banks are jurisdictionally immune to service of process. In the area of privacy, this feature is important to attachment orders or writs of execution, to which private international banks are normally immune. Laws formulated in most international banking centers protect the confidentiality of financial dealings—under no circumstances will the bank divulge that information, even in a lawsuit. In addition, you may also be comforted by the fact that U.S. government demands for information are legally barred by the U.S. courts if such demands would violate the laws of a foreign country.

Thus, even though you, as the bank owner, may be a U.S. resident, the bank is a totally foreign entity, and the law prohibits any attempt to reach it in a legal sense by using you as a conduit (see *United States v. Germann*, 370 F.2d 1019, 1022–23 [2d.Cir. 1967]).

Flight Capital: Fighting
Asset Concentration

In many countries, wealthy citizens have had their assets seized, stolen, or placed under a lien. If you take your nest egg and diversify politically or geographically by going international, you can minimize the vulnerability of your assets.

The unfortunate truth is that America is not exempt from the laws of history. In times of crisis, *all* governments tend to persecute the financially independent by means of price controls, rationing, foreign-exchange controls, prohibition of foreign accounts, confiscation of property, and high taxes. War, or even the threat of it, can precipitate such governmental restrictions.

History has many lessons to teach, obviously. Among these are that discrimination can strike even the most powerful within a society, that both the financial institutions and the governments that prop them up can topple, and that laws can be passed overnight that allow your precious property to be seized—or perhaps even your life. Such things continue to happen all over the world.

This is why smart investors living in politically and socially explosive countries often keep the bulk of their money offshore. Overriding (and rational) fears of government expropriation push them into a no-choice position. As Americans, we may be less fearful, but can we afford to be less prudent?

The obviously prudent course is to act before the fact—*before* any period of unrest can bring you and your assets under federal scrutiny. Once the crackdown occurs, it will be too late.

Privacy of Bank Records

If you had the proper credentials and $50, you could probably gather the following information and material on any individual: checks (front and back copies), bank statements, signature cards, loan applications, deposit and withdrawal slips, and copies of all bank communications. And the person would never know his private records had been obtained without his approval.

Domestic banks typically release records in the event of civil litigation, criminal proceedings, SEC investigations, or IRS audits. Private investigators often pose as officials with federal authority to review bank records. In this way, they are also privy to what you suppose is confidential information.

However, by utilizing a private international bank, you ensure against any such invasion. These records, so easily obtained inside the United States, remain firmly outside the jurisdiction of both the U.S. government and the U.S. courts and the foreign locale usually inhibits non-governmental investigators and other third parties who might be prone to pry into your records if they were in the United States.

In addition, the laws of most private international bank host countries not only protect against any unwarranted attempt to force the disclosure of your bank's records but also provide for punishment (in many havens this includes even a jail term) of anyone who knowingly (or in some cases accidentally) breaches bank secrecy laws.

LOWERING YOUR FINANCIAL PROFILE

I mentioned earlier the wisdom (and difficulty) of keeping to the minimum the information that gets created about you. Obviously, relocating your finances offshore is the best method for reducing such visibility. This private world can shield your major bank accounts, investments, trusts, companies, and other entities.

But what about the rest of you that still resides in the United States (assuming you don't wish to become an exile)? You'll probably want to keep some assets at home. As it happens, there are ways to do that while still protecting yourself from unnecessary invasions of privacy. Here are a few suggestions (burying your cash in a shoebox isn't one of them):

- Look for a domestic bank willing to ensure the highest possible level of financial confidentiality. Despite the strangulating U.S. regulations outlined above, some banks are significantly less intrusive than others. But some of the worst ones have actually started photographing and fingerprinting customers before completing routine transactions. Obviously, you'd be a fool to bank at such an institution. Ask any prospective banker for a written contract that states the ground rules for your professional relationship. Make sure that your agreement states that the bank must notify you whenever anyone asks to see your records and that you reserve the right to periodically see and correct any records the bank may keep on you.

- Be careful in your check writing. Your monthly statement provides a detailed picture of your everyday life—where you shop, eat, and worship; the names of friends and relatives; your political affiliations; and any private clubs you belong to. Limit your checking account use to routine expenses, such as mortgage or rent, utility bills, and car loans. For more sensitive purchases, open and maintain a second account, preferably offshore.

  Even better, handle these through a registered trade name. Simply set up a company and conduct your discreet transactions through its checking account. It's perfectly legal as long as you register your business and use it without intent to defraud.

- Curtail plastic purchases. Just like your checkbook, your "onshore" credit cards provide a detailed diary of where you go, what you buy, whom you telephone, etc. Charge these expenses offshore. But make sure the offshore issuing bank—and I hope it's your own—is in a jurisdiction that has strong banking privacy laws.

- Invest through a registered trade name. Brokerage firms accept corporate accounts, which can be used by individuals as well as by large corporations. A professional corporation can trade under its own name and, if titled properly, will ensure the anonymity of the real owner.

Note: Your privacy is maintained only at the trading level. Outsiders can still gain access if the brokerage firm chooses to reveal the true owner.

- Rent a post office box. Along with a registered trade name, this can provide a significant amount of confidentiality.

Ultimately, of course, "onshore privacy" is an elusive goal, if not an outright contradiction in terms. Only by moving a portion of your assets offshore can you escape excessive government regulation and bureaucratic red tape—and, for the first time in your life, discover what true financial freedom feels like.

CHAPTER 5

TAX PROTECTION BENEFITS OF A PRIVATE INTERNATIONAL BANK

I've mentioned that profit and privacy are the first two P's that motivate my clients to consider offshore banking. The third P is definitely protection—protection *from* excess taxation and protection *of* assets. I'll be outlining asset strategies in the next chapter, but now it's time to talk taxes.

At least half my clients are seeking legal ways to lessen the burden of their tax load. As you may imagine, I'm more than sympathetic. I happen to believe that your money, whether earned as a return on wages or on invested capital, belongs first to you, not the government.

It is ironic when you think that our country was born out of history's most successful tax revolt—and now has the most complicated and burdensome revenue laws in the world, even beyond the understanding of most tax specialists! And, despite all the campaign promises of tax relief and tax reform, our tax rates constantly increase to cover deficits, defense spending, and mammoth, mandated social-welfare programs—with no turnaround in sight. Like that old bumper sticker put it, "The IRS: We've got what it takes to take what you've got."

But let me make my position absolutely clear: *The ability to legally avoid undue taxation does not excuse any American taxpayer from paying taxes.* I'll be even more specific: *The ability to use a private international bank as a means of tax avoidance does not in itself excuse American taxpayers—individual or corporate—from paying U.S. taxes on their share of bank income.*

However, an essential distinction must be made between *tax avoidance* and *tax evasion.* Avoidance means legally taking advantage of the law to keep from paying tax. Any reputable accountant will encourage you to avoid taxation. In fact, if your accountant isn't working with you to plan intelligent tax-avoidance strategies, you better start looking for a replacement.

Evasion, on the other hand, is illegal, involving willful criminal intent to defraud the U.S. Treasury. This includes failure to file any reports generally required of Americans with overseas business interests. It is against the law to hide any percentage of your money—no matter how small—from Uncle Sam (who, of course, thinks it's really his).

But it is not illegal, or immoral, to move your money outside Uncle Sam's sphere of tax authority. Legally constituted and operated private international banks do not evade taxes. However, they can, and legally do, avoid taxes pursuant to the terms and conditions of U.S. tax laws, rules, and regulations by separating you from your money in a way that protects you from the tentacles of the IRS.

For example, the Internal Revenue Code provides for taxation of a parent shareholder on undistributed profits from an ordinary foreign corporation. However, international banks are a special kind of foreign corporation. Because of privileges and exemptions that U.S. tax law grants banks in general, and foreign banks in particular,

It is not illegal, or immoral, to move your money outside Uncle Sam's sphere of tax authority. Legally constituted and operated private international banks do not evade taxes. However, they can, and legally do, avoid taxes pursuant to the terms and conditions of U.S. tax laws, rules, and regulations by separating you from your money in a way that protects you from the tentacles of the IRS.

private international banks can often legally avoid undue taxation on profits derived from the ordinary conduct of banking business.

However, the changing complexity of U.S. tax laws and the uniqueness of each situation make it virtually impossible to discuss a particular tax plan. Planning of this type must be done on a case-by-case basis and constantly refined in accordance with the business dynamics of each private international bank.

But it is certainly possible, and very useful, to outline in a general context the tax benefits associated with ownership of a private international bank.

THE DUALISM OF TAX BENEFITS

First and foremost, it's necessary to appreciate that a private international bank is subject to the tax laws of two jurisdictions: the United States and the host country. Tax benefits in terms of American law generally involve methods of avoidance. Tax benefits in relation to the international jurisdiction generally flow from an absence of host-country income tax or other burdensome government regulation.

With respect to U.S. tax law, the advantages of doing business internationally, particularly banking business, have already been discussed. If there were not material tax advantages to operating outside American jurisdiction, such old-line American companies as Pfizer, Merrill Lynch, and American International Group would never have gone to the expense of establishing international banking subsidiaries.

Diplomacy and Dollars

The taxation issues of international banking are delicate. Obviously, the United States must act as a member in good standing of the international financial community. As such, though the IRS may dislike the idea of international financial freedom for its citizens, it must frequently tolerate it as an accommodation to the sovereignty of various international financial centers.

Corporate Insulation

A corporate structure insulates the personal assets of incorporators because a corporation is, for legal purposes, an entity separate and distinct from the persons controlling it. Likewise, a private international bank is a separate corporation with a legal personality distinct from its shareholders. Stated more simply, an offshore corporation or bank is as much a legal entity as you are. Therefore, to the IRS and other government agencies, its assets, liabilities, and income are its own.

Host countries have a record of preserving on behalf of shareholders the privacy of the international banks they charter. This is the essence of being considered an international haven. Thus, a host jurisdiction may reveal the name of a bank held by American shareholders but not the names of those shareholders or the scope of their financial activities. The personality of the bank is respected by the host country in a way that defends it from IRS interference.

Taxation by International Jurisdictions

Most host countries impose no taxes on profits, income, or capital gains earned by a private international bank. Usually, income-tax benefits are statutory and are the very reasons U.S. shareholders apply for bank charters in the first place. Host countries do charge the bank an annual license fee, which is paid to the government as a business-license fee. A few jurisdictions have a modest reserve requirement as well. If any income tax is levied, it is generally nominal.

SPECIAL STATUS OF PRIVATE INTERNATIONAL BANKS

Because the United States wants to attract foreign money, special tax benefits are available to foreign banks. It is fair to say that, seen from afar, the United States of America is itself an international tax haven. The Internal Revenue Code and regulations yield special tax privileges and advantages for foreign banking corporations. Such privileges are available provided the bank can substantiate that it is conducting bona fide banking business outside the United States.

Once the IRS respects the bank's banking status, the bank may be able to include in its gross income revenue derived from a broad range of financial activities classified as merchant-banking income. Such activities include buying and selling stock as an underwriter; acting as investment adviser, merger consultant, or business manager; or engaging in a broad range of manufacturing and business activities outside the states.

With respect to defining international banks as authentic financial institutions for U.S. tax purposes, the key aspect is sometimes not so much that banking business (borrowing, lending, and investing) occurs but that it takes place on behalf of persons not related to the bank in a material way—in other words, on behalf of persons or companies that are not bank shareholders.

Interestingly, many activities that foreign banks are allowed to conduct in the United States (e.g., buying real estate) are specifically forbidden to domestic banks (Treas. Reg. Sec. 1.864-4[c][5][I]; Treas. Reg. Secs. 1.551.4, 1.552.5).

Exclusion from Controlled Foreign Corporation (CFC) Tax Penalties

If any number of Americans, each of whom owns at least 10 percent of a bank, together own more than 50 percent of a bank, that bank will be classified as a controlled foreign corporation (CFC), and the U.S. shareholders will be subject to current U.S. tax on their share of the bank's earnings, whether those earnings are distributed or not.

However, the Tax Reform Act of 1986 granted a special privilege for foreign banks owned by a single U.S. shareholder engaged in the business of export financing for its parent shareholder. Under this rule, interest income derived from financing exports for the bank's owner will not be subject to the CFC tax penalties.

Should the bank wish to escape the CFC tax penalties without limiting its activities to export financing, it is suggested that the bank's ownership be structured for the U.S. citizens to own less than 50 percent of the bank. Under this type of arrangement, two options are generally available:

1. Establish a bank with a 50 percent or more foreign partner, thus permitting the bank to avoid being classified as a controlled foreign corporation.
2. Establish a bank with eleven or more unrelated persons, each owning less than 10 percent. Again, under this arrangement, the bank will not be classified as a controlled foreign corporation.

In practice, it may be relatively easy to decontrol the bank under these two options. One way is to bring in ten friends or business associates, each owning less than 10 percent. This arrangement has the added benefit of infusing additional capital to operate. Another way might be to offer a stake in bank ownership to ten key customers. This method allows the customer to feel part of the bank while helping to solve the bank's tax problem.

In certain situations, it may be practical to automatically enlist each CD depositor as a bank shareholder. In such a case, a portion of the customer's intended deposit is placed with the bank and the remaining portion used to purchase stock in the bank. With this approach, it is important to monitor all ownership percentages to ensure no American ever exceeds 10 percent.

Exemption from Foreign Personal Holding Company (FPHC) Tax

Shareholders (U.S.) of a foreign corporation more than 50 percent owned by five or fewer shareholders are, in most cases, subject to current U.S. taxes on their proportionate share of passive income from foreign sources (assuming the foreign corporation is not subject to full U.S. tax because it is "engaged in a U.S. trade or business" under the foreign personal holding company [FPHC] provisions of the Internal Revenue Code [IRC Sec. 551]).

The FPHC provisions enable a foreign bank to apply to the IRS for an exemption from FPHC tax, provided it can show it was not created for the express purpose of avoiding the tax. In the IRS's eyes, a private international bank—if it is to obtain the FPHC exemption—must be able to show that it is a duly chartered financial institution engaged in banking business. It is unlikely that a private international bank located in a tax haven will be granted such an exemption (Treas. Reg. Sec. 1.552[b][2]).

Moreover, even if a bank is able to obtain an exemption from the FPHC rules, it will still be subject to the CFC penalties if it is more than 50 percent controlled by Americans, each of whom owns 10 percent or more of its stock. Thus, FPHC status is, in most cases, avoided in the same manner as under the CFC rules—through 50 percent or more foreign ownership or through ownership dispersed among eleven or more unrelated persons.

If an international bank limits its FPHC income to less than 40 percent of its earnings, it can, in most cases, completely avoid the FPHC tax (IRC Secs. 551–555). As a practical matter, however, limiting earnings in this manner is difficult for a bank.

Exemption from Accumulated Earnings (AE) Tax

A foreign corporation is ordinarily subject to U.S. tax at rates of up to 38 percent on undistributed U.S.–source earnings in excess of $150,000 per year. The theory is that accumulated earnings not used to run the corporation are excessive and thus are taxable.

But an ample money reserve is the primary operations tool of a financial institution. Accordingly, a private international bank will usually qualify for exemption because, in the ordinary course of its business, it must accumulate earnings in order to make portfolio investments. Such portfolio investments within the meaning cited in the foreign banking corporation guidelines outlined earlier are considered an activity of a bona fide bank. And, as previously mentioned, banking activity as such identifies the international bank personality, thus qualifying it for special treatment under tax law (Treas. Reg. Sec. 1.532[2][b][5]).

Deferral of Foreign Investment Company Tax

The American shareholders of any foreign corporation—whether a bank or other type of corporation—are taxed on their share of the corporation's passive income if the company's passive income exceeds 75 percent of its total.

However, payment of this tax on passive foreign investment company income can be deferred until the income is actually repatriated. If an election to defer is made, then, once repatriation occurs, the American shareholder pays interest on the amount of tax previously deferred. The rate of interest is the IRS statutory rate or rates on deficiencies during the period of the deferral.

Exemption from U.S. Tax on Foreign-Source Income

An ordinary foreign corporation is subject to U.S. tax on foreign-source income if that income is "effectively connected with a U.S. business." (Treas. Reg. Sec.1.8618).

Regulations in this regard are extensive, and many connections constitute "effective" connections. But a private international bank duly constituted and properly managed outside the United States will ordinarily be exempt from tax under this rule since its activities will be conducted internationally through a resident agent or through host-country directors named in its charter. The international bank must be able to demonstrate the validity of the resident agent as effective principal, while the person(s) deemed to be the primary shareholder(s) might be shown to be the discreet American agent of the bank.

Exemption from Assets-Used or Business-Activities Test for Dividends and Gains from Securities Transactions

An ordinary foreign corporation may be subject to tax on certain U.S.–source dividends and securities gains under the assets-used or business-activities test.

A private international bank, in the ordinary course of conducting banking business outside the United States, will be exempt from U.S. tax under the assets-used or business-activities test. The reason is that it is a financial institution, dealing as a matter of course with securities. It requires that assets derived from income or profits on securities sales be available on a continuous basis so that it may conduct its ordinary activities. The case for exemption is therefore compelling (Treas. Reg. Sec. 1.864-4[c][5][ii]).

Special Tax Treaty Advantages for International Banks

Dividends, interest, and royalties paid to an international bank from U.S. sources are subject to a 30 percent withholding tax. If an international bank earns passive income on American investments and that income is paid to it, the payer has to withhold 30 percent of the amount and remit it to the IRS. Basically, this withholding tax is the income tax that the international payee is giving to the IRS in return for being allowed to do business with an American person or corporation.

If, for example, an American borrower has a loan with an international bank and is making an interest payment, he would pay out only 70 percent of the interest payment to that bank. The other 30 percent goes to the IRS.

Two issues are important here. First, the IRS sees the act of withholding the 30 percent as the borrower's responsibility. In reality, it cannot prosecute a foreign bank but can hold a U.S. borrower liable for the 30 percent, plus penalty. The second aspect is more agreeable. On the one hand, the borrower may use this 30 percent as part of interest-payment deductions on his return. On the other, this same 30 percent may be deducted on a return the international entity may file with the IRS to claim tax benefits—the point being that the IRS may collect this 30 percent only one time.

The ground rules change, however, if the international bank or its financial subsidiary is located in a treaty jurisdiction providing for withholding relief. An American corporation or individual using an international bank in a treaty jurisdiction to borrow abroad can escape the 30 percent withholding tax on interest payments to foreigners and can thus borrow money more cheaply.

In such a case, the withholding tax rate and any reporting requirements or tax credits deriving therefrom are reduced to the amount specified in the tax treaty. The small amount is a nod to international diplomacy, which holds that, between two nations, tax treatment should be fair and equitable. It's a form of "most-favored-nation" status.

With respect to private international banks, the interest-withholding exemption may be associated with the fact that interest, of itself, is deemed an ordinary part of a bank's income or profit. For example, Article III of the tax treaty between the United States and the United Kingdom provides this exemption with supporting authority (Rev.Rul. 72-378; 1972 C.B. 662; 73-354, 1973-2 C.B. 435; Rev.Rul. 65-78, 1965-1, C.B. 630).

The existence of a treaty between the United States and the international bank jurisdiction may, depending on the

> **I**t follows that individual American share-
> holders of private international banks, in
> their capacity as owners of foreign banking
> corporations, may acquire special, advanta-
> geous tax treatment quite unavailable to
> them as ordinary citizens or companies.

treaty, define those factors that give evidence that the bank
has a "permanent establishment" (e.g., office) in the United
States and, thus, has a U.S. trade or business subject to the
full range of U.S. tax law. Without a treaty, the argument
as to what activities constitute U.S. trade or business as
conducted by the private international bank within the U.S.
becomes less clear.

The Bank Charter's Integrity

The principle of private international banking stands up to
close analysis. As a financial corporation, it is the primary,
most usable international business vehicle of maximum tax
benefits. The benefits derive from the fact that a banking
institution is a special kind of corporation. Just as corporations acquire special, advantageous tax treatment in relation
to American individuals—and just as banks acquire special,
advantageous tax treatment in relation to American corporations—so foreign banks acquire special advantageous tax
treatment in relation to American banks.

It follows that individual American shareholders of
private international banks, in their capacity as owners
of foreign banking corporations, may acquire special,

advantageous tax treatment quite unavailable to them as
ordinary citizens or companies.

LEGAL CONSEQUENCES OF TAX BENEFIT

A valid question is whether, over the long term, legal avoidance of tax under the U.S. tax system is possible. The
answer is an emphatic yes, and several cases in point are
uncommonly apt.

Merrill Lynch & Co. Inc. has a strong record of seeking
the most favorable tax treatment available at all levels of
operation and in relation to all levels of government—
federal, state, local, and international. Though its executive
offices are and always have been in New York City, Merrill
Lynch was incorporated in the state of Delaware at a time
when to do so meant it would pay a substantially lower corporate tax than it would in New York.

A recent 10-K of the company is a revealing tax-related
document. Just as the parent company is a Delaware corporation, so are about forty of its U.S. subsidiaries. Among
these is Merrill Lynch International Inc.—and one of this
subsidiary's subsidiaries is an international bank chartered
in a leading offshore haven, known as Merrill Lynch International Bank Inc. This bank in turn owns several other
foreign corporations based in locations that read like a
Who's Who of international jurisdictions: Panama, Hong
Kong, the Netherlands Antilles, Singapore, Switzerland,
Belgium, and others.

It is significant that Merrill Lynch's extensive international holdings are owned by its international banking
subsidiary. In its annual report, the company rather coolly
takes the position that income taxes will never be paid
on the $43 million in undistributed earnings of its for-
eign subsidiaries.

Why? Because this income "will be invested indefinitely overseas." In other words, the money will never be repatriated but will remain a part of the working capital of Merrill Lynch International Bank Inc.

How can Merrill Lynch take such a position? Basically, because it says U.S. law backs it up. The annual report virtually dares the IRS to challenge its stand.

Merrill Lynch's attitude toward tax laws regarding foreign-source passive income is striking because it invokes the very rules it quite legally and properly steers clear of. And it may do this because it can also show that the passive income is controlled by an institution not only engaged in banking and finance but engaged in it well outside U.S. jurisdiction and, thus, engaged with third parties. These three conditions met, the parent company can use and reuse the $43 million with no tax liability whatever.

The IRS isn't auditing the corporate conduct of Merrill Lynch, nor does it appear to be challenging, let alone disallowing out of hand, the assertions made by the company that it need not pay income tax on undistributed earnings.

The future of Merrill Lynch & Co. Inc. as a continuing business, with domestic assets remaining unattached and foreign assets remaining both retained and unthreatened, seems a secure one. Indeed, the position of Merrill Lynch as one of the premier American brokerage and finance conglomerates remains intact.

A suspicious person might think Merrill Lynch was receiving preferential treatment because of its eminence in the American business community and its powerful political contacts. However, if you check the 10-K reports and business practices of hundreds of other public American corporations, both large and small, you'll find similar statements regarding the overseas activities of these companies and the tax stance of their foreign banking subsidiaries.

I quote directly from a recent Pfizer Inc. Form 10-K: "The company wholly owns offshore financial subsidiaries, including Pfizer International Bank. The aim of this subsidiary is to improve the company's profitability by increasing financial flexibility overseas."

That's a fairly subtle restatement of Merrill Lynch's position, but an examination of the figures contained later in the 10-K show absolutely no provision for payment of U.S. taxes on the operations of Pfizer International Bank.

The point is that the legality of the activities of these major U.S. companies appears incontrovertible. Their 10-K reports (and the acceptance of those reports by the SEC) clearly show that U.S.–owned and –controlled international banks allow their parent shareholders to use the banks in order to legally avoid paying any tax that the Internal Revenue Code does not technically require them to pay.

The special tax benefits proceed directly from the existence of the international banking subsidiary—and the same benefits flow to the individual American owners of private international banks.

That is not to say, however, that foreign banks or their shareholders are, in all cases, free from federal income taxation or that the advantages of these offshore tax-avoidance strategies will last forever. After all, the U.S. tax authorities are keenly aware that these international havens offer a perfectly legal way for increasing numbers of enterprising Americans to circumvent confiscatory taxes. But investors who act without delay may still reap incredible tax savings.

A Cautionary Note on Tax Benefits

Potential organizers of private international banks need to be aware that the federal income tax aspects of owning a foreign bank can be quite complex. As such, the tax implications should be discussed with an attorney, accountant, or other professional adviser before a final decision regarding private international bank ownership is made.

CHAPTER 6

ASSET-PROTECTION BENEFITS OF A PRIVATE INTERNATIONAL BANK

I mplicit in the credo of American enterprise is not only the freedom to accumulate wealth and spend it as you deem fit but to leave what remains after your death to your heirs. Unfortunately, it's getting harder and harder to live by that capitalistic credo. We have been witnessing an ongoing erosion of our title to our own wealth—both during our own lives and after.

As a consequence, effective asset protection in the United States, if not exactly extinct, is definitely on the endangered list. After the IRS takes its third or more off the top, other slices of your asset pie are served up to pay state taxes, Social Security tax, gasoline tax, consumer tax, and, of course, estate tax on anything you might be lucky enough to inherit. Then there's the cost of liability insurance and loss—everyday components of doing business for many affluent Americans.

But effective asset protection *does* exist—beyond our borders. And for many people of substance, that happy fact is the strongest argument for developing an offshore financial strategy. Once outside the United States, and beyond the reach of excessive U.S. government interference, there are many ways to safeguard what you have and to use it to make more. (Let me emphasize again that I'm not advocating concealing assets offshore, only protecting them.)

THE ROLLS ROYCE OF OFFSHORE VEHICLES

One strategy stands out from all the rest: the ownership of a private international bank. This is easily the best vehicle for the protection of your personal and business assets, whether the shelter you seek is from the IRS, other government agencies, creditors, competitors, or even an angry ex-spouse on a search-and-destroy mission.

As we saw in the last chapter, a private international bank can play a major role in shielding income and capital gains from U.S. income taxes. However, there are many other areas in which you can be damaged by the prying eyes of the government.

Calling on the same justifications it uses in restricting our rights of personal privacy—namely, "crime prevention" and "national security"—the federal government has devoted vast resources to tracking the movement of personal assets by its citizens.

In fact, each of the six reasons cited by Mark Skousen for maintaining financial privacy apply equally to the protection of personal assets. To review, these are as follows:

1. Protection against discrimination
2. Protection against excessive government

3. Preservation of reputation

4. Protection against damages resulting from divorce, family disputes, and lawsuits (This is the area where asset protection is most important and where private international bank ownership can offer the most protection.)

5. Protection against loss due to exposure to criminal actions (If the nature and location of your assets is public knowledge, you are far more likely to be a victim of robbery, burglary, extortion, or even kidnapping.)

6. Protection against "legal fraud" (The knowledge that you are financially well-off exposes you to pressures and promotions by people whose sole purpose is to strip you of your wealth.)

There are many other reasons for wanting to protect your assets, probably even more than for maintaining financial privacy. But, as with privacy, the government continues to ignore these concerns, passing laws and regulations designed to force disclosure of the size, nature, and location of its citizens' assets, thereby putting those assets at risk.

As the owner of a private international bank, however, you will have many options to both preserve your financial privacy and protect your personal or business assets.

WHY A PRIVATE INTERNATIONAL BANK CAN PROTECT YOUR ASSETS

There are two primary reasons a private international bank can be so effective in shielding assets. First, as mentioned in the preceding chapter, as a foreign entity located in an offshore financial center with strict banking secrecy and

> Once the legal ownership of assets passes from an individual to a foreign entity, such as a private international bank, it becomes extremely difficult for attorneys, forensic accountants, creditors, or others based in the United States to identify the nature or quantity of those assets.

financial privacy laws, a private international bank provides a heavy layer of insulation between the assets of its owner and those who might wish to make claims against those assets. Once the legal ownership of assets passes from an individual to a foreign entity, such as a private international bank, it becomes extremely difficult for attorneys, forensic accountants, creditors, or others based in the United States to identify the nature or quantity of those assets.

In addition, if the original transfer of assets was carefully planned and carried out—and the private international bank set up so that the deployment of the assets is directed by a foreign management company under orders of the bank's foreign directors—it can be virtually impossible for claimants to link those assets to the individual against whom claims are directed.

Second, a private international bank, by virtue of its special banking powers and privileges, can cloak the movement of assets and routinely arrange for their investment or disposition without attracting attention. By contrast, the same functions performed by an individual or a corporation would stand out to anyone familiar with the normal pattern of personal or company financial transactions. Activities involving assets placed in a private international bank are legally beyond the reach of creditors.

How a Private International Bank Can Protect Your Assets

There are a host of nongovernment situations where asset protection can be even more important. In fact, many individuals own their own private international banks solely for one of the following reasons discussed here.

Protection of Assets from Creditors

For the individual or small businessperson, the most common threat to assets comes from creditors. In many cases, those threatened don't realize the scope of their exposure until it's too late. Even without resorting to the courts, creditors can gather a staggering amount of information about you—without your knowledge or consent. And this information can paint an extremely accurate picture of the nature of your holdings, targeting them for possible seizure in any action by creditors to collect on your obligations.

In addition, U.S. banks typically release records in the event of civil litigation, criminal proceedings, SEC investigations, or IRS audits. Nor are domestic banks the only culprits in the assault on your assets. By going to credit bureaus, creditors can obtain information about any major asset you purchased that involved third-party financing. Through the judicial process, they can subpoena ledgers, records, and other documents from you or your business—and from your accountant, banker, or brokers.

Finally, you can be called into court and forced to give testimony regarding the nature and location of your assets.

By utilizing a private international bank, you ensure against most invasions of this type. When your assets have been legally transferred to a foreign entity based in a country with strict secrecy laws, it becomes extremely difficult for creditors, investigators, or others to get the information so readily available from U.S. sources. And, when the assets placed in the bank are controlled and managed by foreign, nonrelated parties, it may prove impossible for creditors to link assets to you even if they are able to identify them.

This buffer of foreign location and foreign direction could protect you even if you are called to testify. While you may have to admit that you have placed assets with a foreign entity, you may truthfully say that you can't identify those assets or control them. And, though you may have to identify the foreign entity or persons who do control the assets, it is highly unlikely the records of the foreign entity or the foreign citizens could be forced to come under the jurisdiction of U.S. courts.

Extra Layers Provide Extra Protection

If the buffer of a single private international bank with international management still leaves you with a feeling of insecurity, you can further insulate your assets from seizure by creditors or other parties by adding extra layers to your offshore protection plan.

For example, you might have your bank in a South Pacific haven file a DBA (doing-business-as) statement, permitting it to operate under a different name, then have your management company register ownership of your assets in the fictitious name.

You might also set up an offshore corporation in a totally different foreign jurisdiction, such as the Cayman Islands, then have that corporation serve as a signatory for your South Pacific bank. Assets could then be transferred to the corporation, which would assign them to the bank, which would record ownership in the DBA name.

This process can be expanded almost indefinitely, with five or six different layers between the point at which you transfer the assets offshore and the entity that is eventually recorded as the owner of the assets. Each layer serves as an additional hurdle for anyone trying to identify and locate your assets—and it legally puts you one step further from control of those assets.

ASSET-PROTECTION BENEFITS FOR BUSINESSPEOPLE

The same protections against creditors that apply to individuals also apply to American businesspeople. But there are numerous other situations where private international banking can offer protection for business assets.

Take, for example, actions by aggressive competitors. If you bank within the United States and become involved in a business lawsuit, a court may give your opponent legal access to your financial records, seriously jeopardizing your legal position. If, on the other hand, your records are kept in a private international bank, they are impervious to court orders. That's because private international banks are jurisdictionally immune to service of process.

The laws of most international banking centers protect the confidentiality of financial dealings and protect banks chartered there from foreign court orders, writs of execution, or attachment claims. Under no circumstances can your private international bank be forced to divulge information regarding its assets or those of clients—even in a lawsuit.

You even get protection from government claims as long as your private international bank has no operations and does no business within the United States. Federal government demands for information from foreign banking institutions are legally barred, if those demands conflict with the laws of the foreign jurisdiction.

Trade-Secret Protection

Other important assets for which a private international bank can provide protection include your ideas. Assume you have a formula or patent you want to protect. If you copyright or patent the idea in the United States, you must disclose it to the Copyright Office. In the process, your million-dollar concept becomes part of the public domain. Before you can establish a firm market, the concept can be reformulated with minor changes and marketed by your competition.

However, instead of going to the appropriate domestic office to file your formula, you can convert it into financial information. Call it "exhibit to an agreement between scientist and the formula's owner." If the formula's owner just happens to be a private international bank, the exhibit is likely to be protected under the bank secrecy laws of the relevant international center.

Protection Against Product Liability Claims

Businesses that conduct their operations through offshore entities such as private international banks may also gain some immunity against domestic liability, even if the products of that business eventually come back into the U.S. market.

This protection was verified in 1987 when the U.S. Supreme Court ruled a Japanese firm could not be tried in California for alleged liability in a fatal 1978 motorcycle accident. The Court concluded that, even though its products were eventually marketed in the United States, the Asahi Metal Company of Japan could not be sued for damages in U.S. courts because the company did not do direct business in the United States. The Court held Asahi could not be expected to defend itself here when it had no operations in this country. The Court also ruled any action by U.S. courts with regard to liability would interfere with the interests of Japanese courts.

Legal experts say this ruling makes it extremely difficult, if not impossible, to sue foreign manufacturers and other types of businesses for product-liability damages.

On the basis of that opinion, a foreign-based business—even one owned by a U.S. citizen—might be able to insulate itself against U.S. liability claims by wholesaling its products to a private international bank, which could then resell them to a U.S. distributor. The business might thus be protected from liability claims because it did not do direct business in the United States, whereas the bank would be protected by virtue of the laws of its offshore jurisdiction.

ASSET-PROTECTION BENEFITS FOR PROFESSIONALS

Professionals—especially doctors and other medical personnel who face the specter of enormous malpractice judgments in U.S. courts—are among the largest users of private international banks solely for the asset-protection benefits.

Malpractice litigation has reached such a level that almost any doctor—no matter how much insurance coverage he has—could be hit with a judgment large enough to strip him of his assets. In 1990, the average general practitioner spent between $10,000 and $15,000 a year on malpractice insurance to cover up to $1 million in award damages. That same doctor today is paying at least $50,000 a year for $3 million of coverage. And medical specialists, such as heart surgeons and orthopedic surgeons, must pay far more.

Doctors used to counter this escalating threat by forming professional corporations and transferring ownership of their personal assets to the corporations. But legal opponents quickly saw through that ploy. Today, almost all malpractice suits target the doctor, his insurance company, and his professional corporation. In addition, the courts have ruled separate holding companies set up by physicians to control their assets can be "cracked" and the assets attached on behalf of a malpractice creditor. This left doctors with little choice but to move assets offshore. A private international bank, especially one with foreign management, is the perfect repository.

Once again, if the bank and assets are controlled and managed by unrelated third parties, it provides a significant buffer between the physician and any malpractice creditor. Even if he is forced to testify that he has placed assets with a foreign entity and identify that entity (which he will no doubt be required to do), he will be unable to define those assets or say how they are being used.

As a result, the creditor will most likely be unable to force disclosure of the size and location of the assets because of the secrecy laws of the private bank's host country—and seizure of those assets to satisfy a U.S. judgment will prove to be impossible.

In fact, if the malpractice suit is frivolous (as too many are), a doctor's mere admission of having the bulk of his assets based offshore could prompt abandonment of the suit or, at the least, a low-cost settlement. The reason is simple. The lawyer will recognize that, even if he wins a full judgment in a U.S. court, he will have considerable difficulty retrieving the assets from the foreign jurisdiction. Accordingly, he may decide there are not enough readily accessible assets to warrant continuing with the suit. Even if he does decide to proceed, he'll likely be much more willing to compromise on a smaller settlement, just to ensure he gets something for his efforts.

Using a Private International Bank to Administer Trusts

Many professionals also employ various types of trusts to protect their assets, using a private international bank as an additional layer of protection against "trust busters."

The most effective approach is to set up what is known as an irrevocable trust, that is, one in which the assets can never be returned to the donor, be that a doctor, an attorney, or another professional. Usually, such trusts are established with the professional's spouse or children as beneficiaries and the private international bank as the trustee. Such a trust is absolutely unbreakable, which means the professional can never change his mind and recover his assets. But, it also means creditors will never be able to attach those assets—even if they can find them in the bank's offshore jurisdiction.

A second popular type of trust—and one where the added buffer of using a private international bank is even more important—is called a "reversionary trust." Such a trust operates exactly as an irrevocable trust, but for a limited period of time (usually ten or more years). Once that time period passes, the assets revert back to the original donor.

A private bank is important in such arrangements because it provides an additional barrier to potential creditors, who can attach the assets of a reversionary trust—but not until it is dissolved, which could be years later. The combined factors of a lengthy delay and difficulty of identifying assets in an offshore location virtually ensure that any potential claimants in a suit, whether for malpractice or other reasons, will find the effort more trouble than it is worth.

Trusts set up through an offshore bank have an additional benefit in that U.S. courts may rule such trusts unbreakable under any circumstances. The key here is proving that you had a legitimate reason (other than avoiding the claims of creditors) for establishing the trust offshore. If that proof can be provided, the court will hold that the trust is outside U.S. jurisdiction and not subject to attack under U.S. laws.

It can, of course, still be attacked in the foreign jurisdiction—but, as already discussed, the laws of most money havens would make the success of such an attack highly unlikely. Another bonus in the case of a reversionary trust is the fact that the assets can legally remain offshore once the trust dissolves and the assets revert to the donor.

One drawback to trust arrangements is that assets placed in trust—as well as the proceeds of the trust if they are not needed for the education or support of the beneficiary—are subject to U.S. gift taxes. The only way to avoid these taxes would be to fund the offshore trust with assets already offshore, but that would almost defeat your purpose since offshore assets already have a large degree of protection from creditors.

Offshore Trusts Can Simplify Handling of Your Estate

Though the transfer of assets to a private international bank offers many protections, it cannot provide protection against U.S. estate taxes. That is because a U.S. citizen is taxed on his worldwide estate, subject to the same exclusions provided for domestic estates. However, by having your assets held in trust by your private international bank, you can avoid probate and thus reduce the red tape and legal expense normally associated with settling an estate. That is possible because the assets under control of the bank's foreign directors could be disbursed directly to your designated beneficiaries as per the terms of the trust.

PROTECTION THROUGH INTERNATIONAL DIVERSIFICATION

As mentioned in chapter 4, wealthy citizens of many countries have lost their personal and business assets or have been prohibited from owning certain assets because of changes in the political philosophy or leadership of their countries. Diversifying your assets politically or geographically in a number of different countries can minimize this risk. And, in these days of worldwide investment markets, it makes eminent sense to spread your assets multinationally, simply to avoid economic upheavals that may beset only one country. Obviously, the more unstable your home country's military, political, or economic system, the more important this tactic becomes.

ONE DRAWBACK: LACK OF BANKRUPTCY PROTECTION

While operating a business or conducting personal financial dealings through a private international bank provide many protections for your assets, there is one area of risk. If your business goes bust or you are forced into personal bankruptcy, the assets you have offshore in a private international bank would not be afforded the protection of U.S. bankruptcy laws.

In most foreign countries, the U.S. concept of bankruptcy protection is not recognized. Thus, foreign lenders, business creditors, and even employees could grab up the assets of your troubled company in a bid to either recover money owed them or gain control of potentially profitable properties.

Sometimes, the actions of foreign creditors don't even make good business sense. For example, when Malcolm P. McLean filed for U.S. bankruptcy protection for his U.S.

Lines shipping company, he hoped to be able to renegotiate his nearly $1.3 billion in corporate debt. Before he could act, however, creditors in the Far East seized four of his huge container ships, valued at $46 million each, and sold them for little more than scrap value. Similar, smaller actions to freeze or seize U.S. Lines' assets also took place in seven other countries, including England, Canada, Italy, and the Netherlands.

Thus, if you run into financial troubles while doing business on an international scale—or your private international bank has financial problems of its own—you will have to personally negotiate settlements with foreign creditors, without the protections U.S. bankruptcy laws.

On the other hand, if you were forced to declare bankruptcy as a result of claims from U.S. creditors, assets that were carefully and legally transferred to the control of a foreign entity, such as a private international bank, could be protected against seizure by those creditors.

AN ASSET CREATED BY PRIVATE INTERNATIONAL BANK OWNERSHIP

You may think of private international banking exclusively as a vehicle for protecting assets that already exist. However, there is one asset that the ownership of a private international bank actually creates. And, though it is often overlooked, it may be one of the most personally satisfying assets you will ever have.

I'm talking about the prestige that accompanies bank ownership—the respect and degree of influence that friends, associates, and even strangers afford you when you own a bank. If you don't believe a bank conveys a sense of power, when was the last time you refused a call from your banker or failed to open a letter sent by a bank? And how much more quickly would you respond to a call from the actual bank owner?

Banks project credibility and substance and exude the mystique of money. It's almost impossible for people to ignore a bank, which is one of the major reasons most private international bank owners become successful. A letter in your bank's envelope gets opened, and a message on your bank's letterhead, signed by you as chairman of a bank, produces action.

Letters from you as president of your own private bank can open doors that might be closed to you as an individual. They can influence government officials or corporate executives, help in obtaining hard-to-get loans from other banks, and attract hundreds of thousands of dollars from depositors anxious to get their money out of countries beset by burdensome taxes or instability.

Thus, one of the most important assets a private international bank protects is the status the bank itself creates.

What about Assets Left Onshore?

To state it without equivocation, the more assets you keep offshore, the greater your protection from all quarters: nuisance lawsuits, the government, and the courts. However, I realize that most people will want to keep some of their assets at home.

How are these best to be safeguarded?

The answer is to combine domestic and offshore protection strategies. For those who have no current claims against them, there are several onshore asset-protection options:

• Unprotected investments may be converted into exempt assets, such as annuities or insurance, which, in many states, are protected from creditors.

- Corporations may hold certain assets safe from creditors. Nevada and Wyoming corporations, for example, offer levels of secrecy protection comparable to many offshore havens.

- Domestic trusts, if irrevocable, can safely hold assets. Revocable living trusts, on the other hand, provide no asset protection.

- Family-limited partnerships, an increasingly popular tool for asset protection, allow you to retain maximum control over partnership assets while providing protection against creditors. The family-limited partnership usually owns most of the family assets (except for the family home, pensions, and IRAs). The husband and wife may be the general partners and thus control the assets. The at-risk spouse, usually the husband, may own only 1 percent of the partnership, thereby entitling his creditors only 1 percent of the distributed profits or partnership proceeds when the partnership is liquidated. The remaining 99 percent of the partnership may be owned by other family members or various trusts, such as a children's trust. An offshore asset-protection trust (see next paragraph) can also be a major limited partner. In fact, a combination of trust, limited partnership, and privately owned offshore bank that serves as trustee can create an almost impregnable financial fortress.

- Offshore asset-protection trusts, properly executed and maintained, can place your assets substantially beyond the reach of any U.S. court and severely limit anyone's ability to enforce a money judgment against you.

A basic foreign asset-protection trust can be set up with anyone as the direct beneficiary, but, for maximum protection, it's better to designate someone other than yourself. You'll also need a trustee: someone to administer the trust and hold its assets for the benefit of the beneficiaries. Again,

Offshore asset-protection trusts, properly executed and maintained, can place your assets substantially beyond the reach of any U.S. court and severely limit anyone's ability to enforce a money judgment against you.

this should not be you; a court is more inclined to invalidate a trust if its creator is also a trustee or beneficiary.

Establishing a foreign asset-protection trust is not terribly complex, but it does require expert advice from a trust attorney.

Of course, this and any other asset-protection strategy needs to be customized to you as an individual, taking into consideration the nature and value of your assets, the perceived financial threat, family structure, and other tax- and estate-planning factors.

A final note: Neither a foreign asset-protection trust nor an international business corporation is as effective in shielding assets as ownership of a private international bank.

CHAPTER 7

MAKING IT WORK:
SOME CASE HISTORIES

Despite the wealth of information given so far on private international bank ownership, you may find it difficult to see how it all applies to you. It may help to show you what others in situations—perhaps similar to yours—have done with their private banks.

In any case, I relish recounting some of the stunning successes of current and former bank owners, both large and small. These real-life examples illustrate how a private international bank can be useful in particular situations you may already have in mind. And I hope they will also spark recognition of other ways a private bank can be of benefit to you.

I've selected a wide range of case histories for good reason. I want to address as many of the areas of potential opportunity (and concern) as possible—from promotion to privacy, from raising capital to safeguarding assets, from tax benefits to generation of profits through both banking and investment activities.

Personally, I find all these stories compelling—reflecting the exceptional nature of the people involved. They provide some fascinating peeks into some lifestyles, which, if not always "of the rich and the famous," are definitely instructive for those of us who may want to move into that general neighborhood.

Two More Offshore P's

In fact, I've been tempted to add a fourth and fifth P—after the three of Profit, Privacy, and Protection—to the benefits of offshore banking. The fourth P could stand for Playground and the fifth for Pleasure (or, in some tropical havens, even for Paradise).

Some of the self-made bankers you'll meet in this chapter stand out because they devised new ways of utilizing offshore institutions. Others are notable because of unique traits, in dress, mannerisms, and outlook. These are true originals, and I'm privileged to have learned something from each of them. A few provide inspiration with their personal stories of triumph over background and long financial odds while others impress with their ability to improve on a well-heeled birthright. Whatever the reason, each tells a tale of creativity and shrewd business instinct. All suggest that, with forethought and proper advice, an offshore bank facility can be established that meets your financial needs.

USING A PRIVATE INTERNATIONAL BANK TO ACHIEVE PERSONAL GOALS

Let me recap—and rephrase—some of these commonly cherished personal goals:

Despite an offshore bank's potential for producing profits—as both an operating entity and an investment vehicle—the majority of people initially become interested in private bank ownership because of other benefits a bank can offer. These people have a personal or business need, and a private offshore bank seems the best way to address that need.

- Increasing one's wealth
- Protecting assets from lawsuits and/or potential liability
- Protecting privacy or keeping a lower profile in order to accumulate toys and property without becoming a financial target
- Lowering one's tax bill
- Gaining increased pleasure from life

Despite an offshore bank's potential for producing profits—as both an operating entity and an investment vehicle—the majority of people initially become interested in private bank ownership because of other benefits a bank can offer. These people have a personal or business need, and a private offshore bank seems the best way to address that need.

While I have hundreds of stories in my files similar to those that follow, these are some of my favorites. There's Nevada gaming tycoon Louis B. Doran, who used a Vanuatu bank to dramatically increase his net worth—and he started with $4 million! Then there's Canadian geologist John Mill Howard, who used his offshore bank to shelter his family's wealth and buy an oil company. And I can't forget Frederico Solis, a charismatic entrepreneur from Acapulco, who used his Anguillan bank to broker loans between big European banks and Fortune 500 companies, netting himself a cool $4.5 million in commissions.

As you'll see, there is a considerable overlap of motivations in these stories due largely to the rapidity with which new private bank owners recognize the true potential of their operations.

Note: In the case of individuals, small ownership groups, or privately owned businesses, I've altered or omitted names to preserve confidentiality.

The Corporation

To establish credibility for our case histories, I'll begin with a story from a corporation mentioned several times earlier, international pharmaceutical giant Pfizer Inc., a Fortune 500 company with stock listed on the New York Stock Exchange.

You would think a worldwide company like Pfizer would be well aware of all aspects of offshore banking, but, as this story proves, even business giants can underestimate the potential of private international banks. Pfizer, which does a large percentage of its pharmaceutical business in overseas markets, decided in late 1985 that having its own international banking entity would help it better manage offshore capital flow and control its tax liabilities.

What Pfizer didn't realize was that its banking arm—Pfizer International Bank (PIB), incorporated in the Cayman Islands and based in San Juan, Puerto Rico—would turn into a major profit center for the company.

Note: The one drawback in this story is the Puerto Rican connection. Pfizer initially selected Puerto Rico because of changes in the island's banking laws designed specifically to accommodate such operations and attract new business. Unfortunately, while the Puerto Rican laws helped Pfizer, they are not currently set up to allow bank ownership by individuals or smaller businesses. Pfizer, by the way, subsequently moved PIB to Ireland, where it became Pfizer International Bank Europe (PIBE).

But in 1986, its first full year of operation, PIB (later PIBE) earned $49 million—more than 7 percent of Pfizer's total profit for the year! It had started with $680 million in seed capital generated by Pfizer's offshore operations. Today, as a result of careful lending policies and astute use of the tax benefits the bank provides, the equity is in excess of $1 billion. Because of the big starter fund provided by Pfizer, the bank didn't make a big effort to solicit deposits, but its fine reputation has brought in a growing flow. And having the bank based offshore removed many of the regulatory roadblocks the company faced with its U.S.–based investments.

The moral of the story: The tremendous success that Pfizer achieved with its private bank can be emulated and replicated—albeit on a smaller scale—by your small business or corporation.

Struggling CPA Earns Big Numbers

Now that you've seen how a private international bank can help out an owner at the very top of the financial ladder, let's drop quite a few rungs toward the bottom—to a single individual with very limited resources but a great idea.

A few years ago, Debra Ashley was a bookkeeper. Today, she is the chief executive officer of her own tax and financial planning firm. She also holds a controlling interest in two other companies: a light industrial firm and a publishing house. As Debra tells her story, she went from a net worth of zero to combined assets of more than $350,000 in only four years—just because she watched what her boss did and figured out ways of doing it better.

Debra worked for the same accountant for nearly nine years and was earning enough money to support herself and two children. But she wanted more of a career. So, while she worked during the day, she went to school at night. In 1991, she passed the state board examination and was qualified as a certified public accountant (CPA). She continued on with the same employer until an attractive opportunity presented itself.

Following up on a suggestion from her ex-husband, Debra contacted Janet, a young accountant based in Phoenix, Arizona. Janet had only recently earned her CPA license and was eager to find an experienced partner. She also liked the idea of working with another woman. It seemed a perfect match. So, in August of 1993, Debra packed her professional certificate, her two small children, a self-defrosting refrigerator, and drove off into a brand-new life.

She liked Janet, she liked Phoenix and the partnership was doing well, but, after two years, Debra decided she wanted to build a more sophisticated clientele for the firm. She contacted some experts to talk about offshore banking, already well aware of its many benefits. Primarily, she was looking for a professional edge over local competitors. She explained that the firm was earning a solid reputation in the city but, because it was run by two women accountants, that it still faced professional discrimination. She was convinced that if she could offer the services of an offshore bank—especially as a means to legal tax protection—she would position herself to handle the most prestigious clients in Phoenix.

She was right. In 1995, with my assistance, Debra acquired an offshore bank facility in Vanuatu. The entire negotiation took just four months and cost her firm only $25,000. Now Debra is well on her way to becoming a nationally recognized businesswoman. Her Phoenix clients enjoy not only a tax haven where their assets are safe but an opportunity to earn handsome interest profits as well.

Debra is a determined person with an innate ability to cut through the babble of everyday conversation and strike deep at the heart of a business matter. Certainly, this has contributed to her success. But Debra's achievements also result from her driving need to be special. She was not born into luxury, nor did early adulthood prove a fairy tale of suburban affluence. Yet Debra wanted the best that life could offer. She decided to get it for herself. Owning and operating an offshore bank is her way of saying, "I've made it."

Big Winner from the "Biggest Little City"

Debra's story shows how a private bank can help breed success when starting from scratch. Now here's a story of a successful individual who used private bank ownership as a vehicle in changing the entire direction of his professional life.

Louis B. Doran was referred to me by a former client, who suggested I write Doran and propose a possible international banking involvement. I made numerous efforts to reach Doran—by letter and phone—but the letters went unanswered and the calls were always received by the same polite but formal secretary, who promised only to pass along the messages.

Then one day I got a call from Doran himself. He said simply that he would be in Los Angeles, where I had my office at the time, for the evening and asked if I could meet with him. His manner was professional yet strangely secretive.

Over coffee in his hotel room, he explained that he was from Nevada and had made his fortune through various gaming and real estate investments. He volunteered financial information without blinking an eye and estimated his net worth to be $4 million. At that time, he held 51 percent of a company that owned, maintained, and operated 200 slot machines and video games in the Lake Tahoe area. He was also the director and part owner of a well-known casino in the Reno area, a full-fledged operation with slot machines, black jack, keno, poker, roulette, craps, a bar, and restaurant. And, of course, he owned a Nevada gaming license.

Over the years, he had seen Nevada change and grow. He seemed utterly at ease with the world of gambling and rather matter of fact about the tremendous wealth he had earned from his involvement with it. But he also confided that he was planning to liquidate his interest in the casino.

"Malls," he said, "are the future." He found them fascinating and had already become a silent investor in two shopping complexes, one of them in Las Vegas. Most recently, he had become involved in a large complex near Carson City, Nevada.

As time went on, he continued to fly to Los Angeles from Nevada—always in the evenings—and would meet with me in his hotel room to discuss details of an offshore bank in the South Pacific. He signed the final papers for his bank in the VIP lounge at Los Angeles International Airport.

The last time we spoke, he said that the International Bank of Vanuatu was doing quite well—that he was using it to handle his investment loans, finance new ventures, escape burdensome onshore taxes, and help him buy a majority interest in three Texas oil wells. He was in the middle of another mall project—this one on the outskirts of Denver—and he was thinking about marrying one of the architects involved in the project. Vanuatu, he mentioned, might be a perfect honeymoon hideaway.

From the Halls of Montezuma to Wall Street

Mr. Doran's case was one of change by choice, but some people are forced into change. In 1986, Gen. Robert M. Shorff suffered a near-fatal heart attack. At the time, he was commanding officer of a Marine Corps base on the East Coast. His doctor's order was plain and simple: Leave the

Corps. After a thirty-year career with the armed forces, he never blinked an eye. He took the order like a trained officer and retired.

Luckily, Shorff had followed the Marine regimen and, for a fifty-four-year-old man, was in excellent shape—except, of course, for the serious heart problem. He took life a little easier, got to know his wife for the first time, moved to the West Coast (not far from Camp Pendleton), and decided that it was time he went into business for himself. By mid-1988, a new venture beckoned. Along with an old friend who once piloted jets for the Air Force, Shorff formed a midsize commercial airline, Air Nevcal. The two men still operate their company, mostly out of the Southwest and Mexico.

It was in the summer of 1990 that Shorff expressed interest in an offshore bank. At our first meeting, a former military attache was at his side, taking notes and staying noticeably silent throughout the meeting. The general estimated his assets at $1.5 million. And, he felt it was time to make a change. He said he wanted to command a financial force that could function internationally. In addition to Air Nevcal, he was involved in a three-way business partnership, Prime Associates, which buys real estate, improves on the properties, and then sells them at a profit. Shorff felt a private offshore bank was the next logical step in his personal investment portfolio.

He had a number of immediate uses in mind. First, he and his partner wanted to establish a second airline, this one to fly routes between the Caribbean and Mexico. They had already contacted interested U.S. investors and had ample capital lined up in Mexico. Shorff was also planning to buy a construction company specializing in the grading and paving of commercial and industrial properties. Counting on influential ties to the Defense Department, Shorff was intending to bid on several government construction jobs. For various reasons, tax avoidance among them, he wanted the offshore bank to act as the agent for the purchase of the construction company. He wound up buying an offshore bank in St. Vincent and, at last report, was doing well with all his ventures.

Dutch Treat: Big Profits from Escrow Accounts

The use of a private offshore bank in planning and developing new business is key, but banks can also be incredibly efficient tools for managing already prosperous businesses—and greatly increasing their returns.

This is the story of the Island Bank and Trust Co., located in the Cayman Islands. It is beneficially owned by a Dutch individual living in Europe. Its business transactions are effected in Europe and, in part, through the bank's U.S. attorney in California. Doing business in a combination of continents does not, in the opinions of the bank owner and of its American attorney, infringe in any way on U.S. tax or banking laws.

The bank is a vehicle within a group of companies that acts as an escrow holder for purchases of real estate in California. Why is this useful? From the time funds are placed in an escrow account in a U.S. bank until escrow closes, they are inaccessible to the parties affected. Only the bank may make use of the money in escrow, and then only in line with the myriad U.S. banking regulations. Furthermore, the American bank, as a fiduciary in real estate transactions, is specifically precluded from investing directly in real estate.

In this case, the owners of the international bank are directly involved in real estate transactions. Because the bank is international and not American, however, it may deal directly in the real estate market. Furthermore, because the escrow bank belongs to the owners, any funds deposited with it may be used according to the owners' priorities.

Thus, the benefits the owners derive are the use of the money during the escrow period and an ability to specify convenient terms for an escrow in relation to the purchase of real estate. Tax benefits are also obtained because the owner of the bank is not a U.S. resident and any short-term portfolio investments made with the escrow funds occur in the bank's name. Any income derived goes to the bank— and is thus tax free.

Note: Another individual, who prefers to remain anonymous, achieved similar success using escrow funds by owning not only a Caribbean-based private international bank but part of a Texas title company as well. In the course of its business, the title company receives substantial deposits and escrow funds for its customers. It maintains a bank account with the international bank, which enables the bank's owner to gain indirect use of the deposits in escrow without the opportunity cost associated with leaving the money deposited with a third-party commercial bank.

Canadian Brings Home the Bacon

In January 1987, John Mill Howard requested information on offshore banks. Howard was a geologist who served as the president of Pacific Resources Ltd., a mining and mineral exploration firm operating in Canada and the United States. He lived in western Canada and wanted to know specifically how he might use an offshore facility to combine personal and business banking. As it turned out, he had organized a small investment company in the late 1960s as a way of managing his family's finances. Through a series of good business decisions and careful reinvestment, he had acquired majority interest in several mining and mineral companies.

When he showed up at my office, he was accompanied by his wife and two grown children: a son and a daughter.

Within minutes it was clear that the Howards were extremely close-knit, and each small decision along the way was tackled through consensus. All four people asked detailed questions and probed until completely satisfied with the answers. The family's financial profile was discussed in great detail.

It turned out the Howards were interested in establishing their own offshore bank as a way of borrowing funds from abroad, namely, from West Germany and France. They were confident further that mineral exploration would reap substantial rewards but needed an immediate influx of capital in order to get the project going. So, the bank's first priority was to target and secure at least $25 million.

Simultaneously, the Howards wanted their bank to manage all other family investments, including two well-endowed trusts. At that time, Howard's personal net worth was $7 million, his wife was worth nearly $3 million, and the son and daughter claimed a combined worth of $750,000. All four would be equal partners in the bank.

Early in 1987, not long after their bank license had been approved, a series of loans was negotiated with two separate European banks. Pacific Resources had already begun exploration of a mine located in Wyoming. With things pretty much settled on that score, the family was starting to use its bank for other, more sophisticated ventures. Howard, for example, has since used the offshore bank facility to purchase a fledgling oil company in Alaska.

From Customer to Bank Owner

There are numerous cases involving people who start off by opening a foreign bank account and soon end up reaching the same conclusion: With a solid background in offshore banking, it's better to establish your own offshore operation than to deposit money in someone else's. It's an evolution of awareness from initial interest and the first foreign account to a thorough investigation of charter and license purchase.

This point was clearly established by a fascinating group of five retired couples, all veteran jet-setters from Newport Beach, one of California's wealthy enclaves. They had initially met one another through a prestigious social club in the area and had subsequently formed a small investment group to handle their personal money matters. The consortium provided a comfortable environment in which they exchanged information and financial suggestions.

For almost four years, they had been investing as a group through an established offshore bank in the Bahamas. They were interested in starting their own facility in either the Caribbean or the Pacific islands. They scheduled a meeting with me and, after learning of the advantages of owning their own offshore bank facility, decided to establish a bank in the Caymans. They liked the islands' international reputation, they could afford the license fee, and the idea of vacations in the Caribbean nicely matched their lifestyles.

Once the initial start-up time had passed, they put their Island International Bank to good use. All their investment holdings were transferred to the bank. They began to save money almost immediately because, instead of paying a transaction fee or other special service cost to a third-party offshore bank, they simply instructed their resident agent to handle all banking matters. They were able to garner deposits from members of their Newport Beach social club, offer attractive interest earnings, and expand their scope of investment opportunity to the international market.

USING PRIVATE OFFSHORE BANKS TO PROFIT FROM THE BANKING BUSINESS

So far these "offshore stories," with the exception of Pfizer, have dealt with people or companies outside the mainstream of the banking business. But I know of many cases involving people or corporations already in the banking or financial business, people with the knowledge to expand opportunities in private offshore banking well beyond what you've already read. Their stories further demonstrate the power and potential possible with private international bank ownership.

One of the most amazing things I've discovered in my consulting is how many banking professionals, both foreign and domestic, are well aware of the value of offshore banks and how they can be used to augment their current banking business.

Profitable Change of Career

One such person was a man of substantial means living on the East Coast. He also happened to be chairman of a modest-size domestic commercial bank. Initially, he bought an offshore bank solely on his own. However, after the bank was organized, he promoted it to a group of investors who became participants. This provided significant tax advantages since the bank could no longer be deemed related to any one person.

The bank is used by the group as an investment vehicle so that portfolio investments in T-bills and other securities may be made in the bank's name. The bank further provides financial accommodations to each owner in the form of credit based on the accrued earnings associated with a proportionate share of each owner's profit.

The bank has gained most of its business from a group of people who belong to a country club of which the promoter is also a member. Transactions are effected through the resident agent, thus preserving the international character of the bank.

Family Heritage Discovers Offshore Banking

An almost identical scenario developed with a man named Darrell Cass Taylor III. He is the picture of old American aristocracy—the essence of East Coast propriety. He is also the chairman of several modest-size banks in upstate New York. Aside from shepherding these red-carpet institutions, his one great hobby is his men's club—no ordinary gentlemen's gym, but a venerated tradition. (In his old-fashioned way, Mr. Taylor probably sees it as the single refuge from a world gone more than a little haywire.)

A man of inner sanctums, where hushed voices and thick carpeting comfort the city's "old money," Mr. Taylor appreciates the quiet ambiance of tax havens. An offshore center's serenity and privacy appeal to him. As a result, when he decided to contact me about setting up an offshore bank, he had already done a bit of initial legwork and was certain he wanted it based in the Mariana Islands. He also knew six members of his men's club who were ready to form a small investment consortium. Since Mr. Taylor was an experienced onshore banker, the offshore enterprise would allow him to capitalize on his expertise.

After all the papers were drawn and duly filed with the proper authorities, he flew off to meet with his new resident agent. After returning from the Pacific, Taylor met with a few more personal friends and wound up with an eleven-member consortium. Their combined deposits amounted to well in excess of $10 million. All of them held CDs guaranteeing 21 percent interest (this was back in 1981, at the height of the interest-rate cycle). Taylor, in turn, was using their funds to purchase various money instruments such as T-bills, bankers' acceptances, commercial paper, and other money market obligations.

In this consortium's case, interest was never paid. Instead, the depositors maintained assets on account and let their money accrue. In the process, they avoided all tax on their earnings. The result was so rewarding for the depositors that, in the spring of 1982, another of the club members who had joined the consortium also contacted me. Though happy with Mr. Taylor's arrangement, he had come to recognize the opportunity in private international banking and wanted to buy his own bank so he, too, could seek out depositors.

From Acapulco with Love—and Money

Of course, you don't have to have any personal involvement with the banking business to recognize how lucrative certain aspects of it can be. That was the case with Frederico Solis, a Mexican industrialist and brilliant businessman who, when he first contacted me, already had a net worth of $1 million for each of his thirty-one years of age. He was very direct, and he had a very clear plan in mind for what turned out to be a highly profitable offshore banking venture.

Solis was interested in establishing an offshore bank that would serve as the intermediary for people he called "the big boys," meaning the largest U.S. corporations and the biggest banks in Europe. His idea was completely original and one that taught even me an entirely new way of using offshore banks.

First, he would garner potential borrowers and then advise certain banks of their interest as a way of attracting sizable lenders. He reasoned that if an offshore facility were able to attract big-name borrowers—for example, the Fortune 500 companies—it would automatically attract big-name lenders, such as Union Bank of Switzerland, Barclays, and Credit Commercial. He was right!

The first step in Solis's plan was to obtain financial mandates from several multinational corporations. With his Swiss-American Bank fully chartered and licensed to do business in Anguilla, he began work. Introducing himself as the Mexican representative for the Swiss-American Bank, he would schedule luncheon appointments with treasurers of various Fortune 500 companies. After sundry business preliminaries, he would get to the real point: He could offer each treasurer lower borrowing rates than they were finding elsewhere. Needless to say, few doors slammed in his face.

Within ninety days, he had ten letters in hand. Each had been signed by a treasurer, and each indicated that a major corporation was looking for funds at some specific interest rate. Solis then flew to Europe and approached the leading banks on the Continent. He later explained that he made it a rule never to meet with anyone but an institution's top executive. The results were impressive: Virtually every banker committed himself to extending loans—at the rates Solis had quoted to the Fortune 500 corporations.

By using his offshore bank as a broker for the loans, Solis negotiated a small commission on each financial package. With every loan amounting to at least $15 million, his combined commissions were sizable. After just one year of such negotiations, his profits amounted to $4.5 million!

The Brokerage Twist

Many bankers also view private international banks as a means to enter other areas of financial operation from which they are excluded by U.S. banking regulations.

I know of numerous cases where domestic bankers organized offshore banks because they had domestic customers who wanted brokerage services, which their banks were not permitted to provide. (This situation has changed to some extent, though there are still many services from which banks are excluded.) By shifting the accounts of those clients to offshore banks, the bankers involved were able to satisfy customer needs—and create an additional profit center in the process, complete with offshore tax advantages.

Several other domestic bankers have also gone offshore to gain the ability to administer U.S.–based trusts for foreign beneficiaries. In one case, a group of California bankers manages U.S. investments for a Belize trust company—but they do so through a private offshore bank in the Caribbean. Most of the actual transactions for the trust take place internationally, but the arrangements for the transactions are effected in California, a situation that would be difficult if the foreign trust's investments were managed by a domestic bank.

Even Swiss Bankers Go Offshore

For many years (though no longer), Switzerland was considered the epitome of offshore banking centers, but that doesn't mean Swiss bankers never feel the need for foreign banking facilities, as Renato Orelli can testify.

Orelli is from Lugano, a small lakeside city in Switzerland at the foot of the Alps on the southern border with Italy. He remembers growing up on stories of Swiss banking and being thrilled by the mystery of secret numbered accounts held by rich exiles and exotic refugees. He also remembers that bankers, in their dark suits and homburgs, were among the city's most respected public figures. He liked their stern reserve and imagined the conversations they must have had in large rooms of dark wood and rich red leather. While his friends dreamed of joining the circus, Renato envisioned taking his place in this more stately, financial arena.

To make his dream a reality, he studied first in Basel, then in Rome. Later, he worked three years with a family friend: a banker in Toronto. He then returned to Switzerland. By this time, he had realized he wanted not just to be a banker but to be a very special sort of banker. He wanted to provide Old World service, establish close relationships with his clients, and familiarize himself with their investment needs.

Step by step, he built an impressive Swiss banking career. For six years, he served as the manager of a small bank in Lugano. The position allowed him to construct an image of cautious intelligence and calculated initiative. When he left the bank in 1978, he joined four other investors who were forming their own bank. They established one of the most sophisticated institutions in Switzerland. Within a few years, Finanvest Banca was offering a wide range of ultramodern financial services, delivered in the manner of Old World banking.

When Orelli turned his attention to the offshore sector, he was already a widely respected international banker with a high level of expertise, but he still sought out help from several U.S. experts (including me, I'm happy to say), hoping to further expand his professional knowledge. He was, at that time, involved in several investment ventures and had been appointed the director of six joint stock companies in Switzerland. Though he was a bit evasive about his total financial worth, his assets almost certainly topped $3 million.

Specifically, he was eager to establish an offshore bank in association with a few longtime friends. Evidently, they had been involved in a number of past investment opportunities and enjoyed the nature of consortium activity. Orelli was clearly in charge of all details. Within a matter of hours, he had decided on a jurisdiction (Netherlands Antilles), a name (Swiss Credit International Bank), and a number-one banking priority (to obtain financing for a textile factory in Shanghai). Within weeks, he had put together a large group of European investors and had solidified the entire transaction.

Orelli says the offshore experience has proven to be all he had hoped for, and Swiss Credit International has moved into a variety of other offshore banking and financial services, including managing extensive real estate holdings for clients in Europe, Canada, and the United States. And he is making more money from his offshore activities than from his Swiss banking operations.

Silver Spoon Turns Gold

Gil Jameson was an impressive young man with an athletic build and a long-range financial game plan. His family had been in investment banking in the Midwest for three generations, so, as he put it, "Banking is in my blood." Gil was also a world-class polo player.

"People may think polo is an idle hobby," he told me, "but it can get pretty hairy out there. I compare it to soccer or hockey. Those ponies get going around thirty miles an hour—and we're talking collision courses."

Despite his privileged background (or maybe because of it), Gil showed early signs of business initiative. He converted his boyhood baseball card collection into a lucrative investment. Gains from a high school stock-picking club provided him the down payment for his first commercial real estate purchase.

After attending one of my seminars in 1994, Gil decided that, with his family background in banking, owning an international bank would allow him to move much faster toward his goal of becoming a major player in resort-property development.

Did this young man have the "right stuff" to become world class in offshore banking and real estate development as well? My gut instinct told me he did, and I had no trouble buying into his vision and enthusiasm as we worked together to set up his bank.

My instinct was right. Marino Bank (named after Gil's favorite football quarterback) was an almost instantaneous success. It was chartered in Vanuatu, even though Gil intended to specialize in the Caribbean and Florida. Within a few years he had acquired an impressive clientele with an average on deposit of $75,000.

Because of having the bank, and because of other financial structures he put in place, Gil and two subsequent business partners were able to make some major real-estate acquisitions rather quickly. They purchased a hotel near

Daytona for only $75,000 at 6.1 percent interest and had it upgraded from a room to a suite hotel. After doing that and paying a $45,000 franchise fee, they had the hotel appraised for $11.1 million. "It was quite a coup," he recalled proudly.

Another commercial project followed in Panama, a 400-unit development of seasonal rentals. Gil's group sold out the initial two phases (out of four) in six months instead of the year and half that was predicted. For a $500,000 investment, Marino Bank netted around $5.6 million.

In fact, every time Gil and I touch base, it seems he's got another success story for me. He has, for example, just started his own insurance company, selling casualty, life, and annuities, and is in the process of organizing a trust company. The last time we talked, he told me proudly that an international money market fund he plugged his customers into had just blossomed into a number-one-rated fund.

"Having the bank, we were able to open a lot of doors that we wouldn't be able to open otherwise," he says. "But I wouldn't want to anyone to think it has come without effort. There have been a few bumps along the way. But if it was a piece of cake, everybody would be doing it, and owning a bank wouldn't have that special, door-opening value."

The Best Stories Are Yet to Come

An offshore bank charter and license may seem like just another extravagant purchase or, at best, an exceptionally creative investment. But, in fact, they are more than that. The move offshore and the commitment to your own private bank will inevitably mark a new phase in your life. Financial opportunities will expand, and almost without realizing it, you will forever change the way you look at money and how it works.

Which is a way of saying that the most intriguing offshore-banking story has yet to be told. And that next story may be yours.

QUALITY PROMOTION CAN BE
THE KEY TO YOUR SUCCESS

By now, I hope you can see many ways in which a private offshore bank can meet your personal, business, or investment needs. However, if you are like many potential bank owners, you may feel that those individual needs are not great enough to warrant ownership of a bank. Or you may feel that you cannot make an offshore bank a roaring success without attracting additional investors and depositors. And perhaps you doubt your ability to do that. However, in my experience, such doubts are generally groundless. The key to attracting the business you need is quality promotion—an art almost anyone can master (or achieve with outside help from those who have mastered it). And I have several more case histories to prove it.

Start with a Simple Letter

A new bank owner may need little more than a few well-developed letters to bring in a substantial deposit or investor base for his institution. That's because letters from banks command attention. They can open doors, wield influence, and produce millions in deposits for a bank. Private international banks outside the United States are now successfully attracting millions in deposits from U.S. investors and businessmen seeking assured privacy and tax protection. Here is a sample sent out by one offshore bank (the name is changed to preserve confidentiality) to those who browsed its Web page and requested further information:

Other types of letters from your bank—while not directly bringing in investors or depositors—can also have an extremely high promotional or business value. For example, they can enhance your credibility and help you, your associates, or your clients obtain hard-to-get loans.

COMMERCE BANK LTD.
(letterhead)

Dear Sir:

Your Certificate of Deposit account in our bank can now earn you up to 12% tax free. This is considerably more than you might earn through any U.S. bank today. Moreover, your account is maintained in utmost privacy. Under the local banking laws, it is strictly forbidden to divulge information concerning you or your account to any government or tax authority. Current rates paid by our bank on Certificates of Deposit are:

12%: 3-year CD	11%: 2-year CD
10%: 1-year CD	9%: 6-month CD

Your deposit may be sent directly to us by mail—safely and with absolute secrecy. And with the assurance that your account will be serviced with the highest standards of professionalism. More and more Americans are opening accounts with Commerce Bank as a result of increasing U.S. government penetration of U.S. bank accounts. We welcome your business, and invite you to mail your deposit—in confidence—via the postage-paid reply envelope enclosed.

Very truly yours,

(Signature)

Chairman

They can give you access to privileged credit data on competitors, potential borrowers, and others about whom you need information. And, perhaps most important, they can give you access to political and corporate leaders and influence those leaders. Following is the text of four letters designed to achieve these varied goals.

Loan Requests

This is to introduce Mr. John Doe, a valued customer of Bank of Commerce. Mr. Doe has been known to this bank since November of 1984. Both his business and personal accounts are handled in a very satisfactory manner. Mr. Doe is seeking a real estate loan in the approximate amount of $400,000. Unfortunately, as much as we would like to serve him in this area, our bank does not maintain a mortgage loan department. For this reason, we have recommended that he contact your bank, and ask that you extend him every consideration.

Obtaining Credit Information

We are revising our credit information on the XYZ Corporation. Therefore, we would greatly appreciate receiving your comments about the management and financial stability of the company. In addition, we would appreciate receiving your loan experience information, including the present line and high credit. This information will be held in confidence, and we will be pleased to return your favor whenever you have need of similar information.

Requesting Free Product Samples

We have just received your brochure regarding your product known as the Handy Widget. It occurs to our committee that this product may prove to be quite valuable for use by our branch and by other branches that we may be planning to open. Since the acquisition of this product will require a significant investment by our bank, we would like to receive a sample for test purposes. If your product fulfills the promise suggested in your brochure, we will be able to use it. Please be good enough to provide quantity prices, and a sample, at your earliest convenience.

Influencing Political Figures

Our bank is privileged to have a number of wealthy depositors who are known to be active in their support of political candidates. One of these depositors, Mr. John Doe, will be in Washington during the week of March 20. We would be most grateful if you might arrange to receive him in your office for a few minutes one day during that week. Mr. Doe will phone your office within the next week in the hope of confirming the brief meeting. Mr. Doe is an especially valued customer of Commerce Bank, and I think you will find the few moments you meet with him time very well spent. Thank you for your courtesy.

Finding a Niche—and Filling It

Another way to make your bank a success once you've satisfied your own personal or business needs is to find a

> **A**nother way to make your bank a success
> once you've satisfied your own personal or
> business needs is to find a special customer
> need and fill it.

special customer need and fill it. At least that's the advice of
some of America's biggest banks and corporations that also
have private offshore banking operations. Officials of these
companies (with names like Manufacturers Hanover Trust,
Chase Manhattan, American Express, and Citibank) have
all publicly agreed that their institutions would have never
been successful with their ventures into private offshore
banking had they not found a niche—a specific group of customers to which they could tailor their services.

The original concept of private banking, at least as conducted by major banks, involved providing special services
for wealthy clients, the so-called old money of Europe and
the East Coast. But the new breed of private banking that
has come to the forefront in the 1980s and 1990s couldn't
depend on old money. "To get old money, you had to be
around a long, long time," explained one official.

Instead, the new institutions making a move into private
banking in the 1980s had to look for new money. Some targeted the "yuppies" seeking offshore tax relief and investment opportunities. Others went after the venture-capital
markets, providing entrepreneurial financing no one else
wanted to handle. And many focused on the so-called flight
capital market, seeking to serve the needs of wealthy individuals from Third World nations who were afraid of instability in their own countries.

"Each of these groups of individuals has very definite
ideas about where they want to be and how they want their
money managed," explained the vice president for private
international banking at Manufacturers Hanover. He said

even an organization as large as his couldn't adequately serve the needs of so many diverse groups, so "we had to find a niche and go after clients that fit that niche. You don't build a private banking business just by going and randomly knocking on doors."

In all likelihood you will have no desire to make your own private international bank competitive with Manufacturers Hanover or Chase Manhattan—but that doesn't mean you can't use the same methods as these financial giants to make your bank a success. As a new bank owner, you can assess the merits of your bank—everything from location to assets—and the services it can offer. You can then target the market segment most in need of those services. After all, if it worked for American Express, why can't it work for you?

Making a Dream Come True

One of my favorite case histories involves a man named Jim Straw (you may have run across his name before since he's an established writer and publisher). Jim's dream was to own his own private international bank and make it the most successful such bank around. As already amply illustrated, owning a private offshore bank is hardly an impossible dream—almost anyone with some discretionary funds can achieve it. But owning a special bank—one that's a tremendous success—is a bit more difficult. However, Jim did it, and he started the same way you would: by buying a bank.

He set it up in the Mariana Islands and named it First American Bank Ltd. Then he began exploring ways to make his bank a success and found the best way by simply applying his own professional talents. As publisher of a newsletter catering to investors and entrepreneurs, Jim felt he should be able to discreetly "cross-sell" his banking services to his readers, and he did. By running articles about private international banking, outlining the opportunities and advantages and talking about his own experiences as a private banker, Jim increased his readers' interest in the subject.

Soon he was fielding a large number of calls from people wanting to do business with his bank—and it cost him nothing since all promotional expenses were covered by the subscription fee people paid for the newsletter. And, because he was bringing in customers by means of a paid-circulation newsletter rather than having to solicit the general public, Jim avoided entanglement with banking regulators. He has been using the same approach for more than three years now, and it has made him a fortune.

That's not the whole story, of course. Even quality promotion won't keep customers if the bank fails to offer services people want at terms that are truly competitive. Recognizing that fact, Jim developed a comprehensive program for First American Bank customers. His bank pays from 5 percent, compounded daily, for a regular savings account, all the way up to 14 percent for a five-year term account. One-, two- and three-year term certificates are offered at rates in between.

How is Jim able to provide such outstanding rates compared to others available today?

"Simple," he explains. "We keep our overhead low and we do business—not just banking. We have a tightly knit team of people with more than sixty-five years of combined experience in finance, credit, collections and money management. And because we are small, we can move like greased lightning to take advantage of deals that would have to go through a bevy of subcommittees, committees and boards at other institutions.

"This means we can turn our customers' money over faster and get maximum profits on each deal. In addition, while other bankers are restricted in the types of business they can be directly involved in, we are not. We can, and do, get involved in everything from factoring to leasing to wholesaling to manufacturing to publishing—and that gives us a tremendous advantage over other bankers, who are locked in to lending and a few other paper-shuffling endeavors."

The hallmark of Jim's philosophy—and, by reflection, the philosophy of his bank—is integrity. He personally guarantees every penny deposited in his bank. Does that sort of approach work? You bet it does! That's why the heads of Chrysler Motors, Remington razors, and Anheuser-Busch have all gone on television offering their personal guarantees for their companies' products. It converts a cold, faceless corporation into a name and a warm smile.

It's been quite a few years now since Jim Straw set up his private international bank—and both are doing fine. In fact, things are going so well that he often gets asked, "If you're making that much money, why are you paying me only 14 percent?"

You Can Do It, Too

Everyone loves a success story, and the sampling collected here illustrates some of my pet theories about private international bank owners. One is that money has the uncanny ability to draw people out of their shells and open them to new possibilities. Every week, in fact, I hear about international investors and their real-life banking stories—which repeatedly make one clear point:

While each person is different—with individual priorities, worries, and ambitions—virtually all of you reading this book have the intelligence, ingenuity, and drive to make a private international bank serve not only your own needs but those of more than enough investors and depositors to make a bank a profitable offshore investment in its own right.

CHAPTER 8

RISK FACTORS IN PRIVATE INTERNATIONAL BANKING

N o discussion of ownership of a private international bank would be complete if it omitted possible risk factors. In chapter 6, I discussed at some length the fact that assets kept in a private international bank are not protected by U.S. bankruptcy laws. But what other aspects of offshore bank ownership, you may wonder, constitute apparent risks?

There are several, all requiring close examination. As you might imagine, I have made a diligent study of these risk factors for nearly two decades. I have not only reviewed these factors with authorities in all aspects of offshore banking but also surveyed the many private international bank owners with whom I have come in contact (not all of them my clients, by any means). And I have been gratified to find that my own conclusions on the subject echo those of almost every responsible individual or organization involved in offshore banking.

Almost without exception, they all deem the risk factors discussed below to be either nonexistent or bearable since appropriate steps can be taken in advance to minimize financial exposure. In all cases, the benefits associated with owning and operating a private international bank were deemed to outweigh any potential risk.

Possible Infringement of U.S. Law

If a private international bank does business to a significant extent within U.S. borders, the bank and its owners may be restrained by a U.S. court from operating there.

This exposure becomes apparent if the bank is conducting an active trade or business in the United States. For one thing, the bank subjects itself to full U.S. taxation. Bank regulators may also accuse it of banking without a license.

An example of this might be maintaining a rented office on a well-traveled street or placing large display ads in newspapers such as the *Wall Street Journal*, which, incidentally, is only too happy to accept payment for advertising space from virtually any source at virtually any time. The paper has a history of raking in money from companies that advertise with it in good faith, only to later assist various regulators in their investigation of the affairs of those advertisers. But, as has already been stated here several times, it is currently illegal for U.S. owners of private international banks to advertise in the domestic financial media.

On the basis of their own positions and interests, U.S. regulators are likely to raise a number of other potential areas of exposure for offshore bank owners. Some that you may typically encounter include the following:

- From state banking departments—the argument that the bank is conducting business as defined by the state's banking statutes, but is not licensed to do so
- From the IRS—the contention that the bank is subject to full tax treatment under U.S. tax law, either because it is not a bank or because it is conducting a trade or business within the United States
- From the SEC—the claim that the bank is issuing, selling, or otherwise trading in unregistered securities

How to Avoid Regulatory Risks

The easiest way to prevent running afoul of these claims by regulators is to anticipate them—and take appropriate advance measures, such as the following:

- Consulting with a competent attorney familiar with the three types of law involved, that is, state banking, federal banking, and federal securities (The attorney should be familiar with what activities may or may not be performed by foreign banks in a given state.)
- Dealing to a great extent through a foreign-based private bank management company, a resident agent in the country where the bank is based, or an international board of directors
- Adhering to strict procedures designed specifically to prevent each transaction from conflicting with U.S. law
- Developing a good working understanding of what your private international bank can and cannot do within the United States

- Accumulating documentary evidence that can substantiate claims that your private international bank is operating as a bona fide financial institution duly chartered under the laws of the host country

POLITICAL RISKS

Another area of potential risk involves the possibility of changes in attitude or policy by the government of the country where your bank is located. Though I've called it a political risk, this can also be defined as any act performed by a host jurisdiction that affects the private international bank's authority or ability to operate. Such acts can be overt—varying in degree from the enactment of legislation that inhibits the bank's operation (the slightest case) to the nationalization of the ownership of a bank (the severest case)—or they can be indirect, such as the troubles brought on Panamanian-based private international bankers from 1987 to 1989 prior to the ouster of military strongman Gen. Manuel A. Noriega.

In reality, the risk of nationalization or expropriation of assets is considered small in those countries that accommodate private international banking. In order to attract international bankers—and the money they will pump into the host country—offshore financial centers have a standing policy of encouraging free enterprise and tax-haven interest. Either nationalization or expropriation is antithetical to these concepts. It is in the economic interest of host-country governments to refrain from self-defeating regulations.

The risk associated with nationalization and expropriation is apparent only in countries that impose high tax rates and burdensome regulations on their banks. Iran is such a country, as is the United States.

On a lesser scale, yet perhaps more apparent, is the possible enactment of restrictive or inhibiting legislation that directly affects private international bank operation. Once certain international tax havens mature economically or politically, they may become as ossified as tax-heavy countries. Switzerland and the Bahamas have gradually enacted such restrictive legislation and, as a result, have steadily become less attractive as tax havens.

Usually, such legislation results from shortsighted greed on the part of host governments—a tendency by entrenched bureaucrats to "kill the goose that lays the golden egg." However, it can also be the response of an indignant host government stung by publicity or foreign pressure as a result of the misuse or mismanagement of tax-haven privileges by the beneficiaries of those privileges.

The black eye received by some nations that have recently been identified as playing host to financial swindlers, inside stock traders, or money-laundering drug traffickers illustrates the latter point.

A recent and embarrassing example was the European Union Bank, which was incorporated on the Caribbean island of Antigua and offered rates *up to ten times higher than those at other banks!* That alone was enough for the Bank of England to issue a "too-good-to-be-true" warning. But millions of dollars poured in from heedless depositors all around the world. Then, in August 1997, the bank's two Russian-born owners disappeared, and the European Union Bank went into receivership, leaving depositors high and dry—and the island of Antigua with considerable egg on its financial face.

Possible Areas of Regulatory Legislation

Host countries can impose inhibiting legislation on private international bankers in five ways:

1. Increase taxation
2. Adopt financial status disclosure requirements regarding a bank's internal affairs
3. Establish reserve requirements
4. Require a substantial cash deposit with the host government in order to operate
5. Remove the protections against disclosure of the identities of bank customers

How to Avoid Political Risks

Fortunately, there are a number of steps you can take to protect your private international bank against exposure to such risks:

- Select an offshore jurisdiction with a long-standing policy of encouraging free enterprise and international banking. For example, the British colonies have anunparalleled record of stability in this area, which makes many of the British territories ideal sites for private international banking operations.

- When your bank accumulates large amounts of cash, keep that money invested rather than on deposit with international center commercial banks.

- Establish a second private international bank in another jurisdiction as a contingency against possible inhibiting legislation in either location.

- Stay informed of political, social, and economic developments in the host country that could affect your bank. Pay particular attention to potential changes in tax or disclosure laws.

- Support measures requiring the host government to maintain existing secrecy policies and continuously make recommendations to the government for improving its legislation.

BREACH OF PRIVACY RISKS

For international bankers, who rely in great part on privacy, the possible breach of confidentiality is an ever-present risk. I've addressed this issue at considerable length in chapter 4, but I mention it again to underscore that privacy is a precious commodity. Spies, infiltrators, and *agents provocateurs* have occasionally been known to breach tax-haven privacy, at times developing inside sources to tap confidential information that is then sold to the highest bidder. Such sources can range from top host-government banking officials to a single corrupt bank clerk. Equally damaging is the inadvertent breach of privacy that results from poor security, shoddy record keeping, or a slip of the tongue in a casual conversation.

How to Avoid Breach of Privacy Risks

Most precautions in the privacy area involve common sense and sound bank-management practices. However, there are a number of steps you can take to protect against both internal breaches and external or legislative intrusions:

* Don't keep all the pertinent information regarding your private international bank and its customers in one place. It is important to develop methods of record keeping that will give you the financial information you need to operate your bank efficiently and profitably while protecting your confidentiality.

* Deal with resident agents and directors on a need-to-know basis. Provide only information relevant or pertinent to effecting a specific transaction. At the same time, pay all employees or agents enough to maintain their loyalty.

* Screen persons with access to secret or proprietary information for loyalty. Trust no one who has not been screened.

- Use paper shredders when possible. This is a good way to eliminate useless or confusing financial records.
- Constantly test and retest your security.
- Do business in several international banking centers to diversify your risk of disclosure.

Tax-Related Risks

The character of tax-related risk in private international banking arises because formation of such a bank is, in large part, aimed at tax protection. The IRS is constantly attempting to inhibit tax benefits by asserting that private international banks are legally constituted financial institutions only to the degree that banking and financial services are made available to the members of the public unrelated to the bank's shareholder(s).

In effect, the IRS has imposed on the private international banker the need to act as public trustee even while insisting that he has no such status. As such, the U.S. taxing

The character of tax-related risk in private international banking arises because formation of such a bank is, in large part, aimed at tax protection. The IRS is constantly attempting to inhibit tax benefits by asserting that private international banks are legally constituted financial institutions only to the degree that banking and financial services are made available to the members of the public unrelated to the bank's shareholder(s).

agency will employ such tactics as allowing tax benefits for bank activities related to outside parties while disagreeing with your contention that the bank deserves those same tax benefits for operations conducted in its own interests. The IRS may also employ the threat of an audit in a bid to force a bank owner to agree with its contentions, even though it is aware of prior cases where such private-bank tax benefits have been upheld.

How to Avoid Tax-Related Risks

Your risk of getting into trouble with taxes can be reduced by the following prudent measures:

- Stay abreast of constantly changing tax laws both in the U.S. and in the international jurisdiction. When analyzing the relative benefits of various offshore financial centers, note the jurisdiction's record of integrity with regard to respecting the confidentiality of private international bank owners, their customers, and their financial transactions. (Again, the British colonies have a strong record in this area.)
- Carefully analyze all financial transactions with a view toward eliminating tax liability. Structure your bank's financial philosophy and individual deals accordingly.
- Observe the uses to which potentially inhibiting U.S. tax regulations are put by such major companies as Merrill Lynch, AIG, and Pfizer. Look at major U.S. "industrial" corporations involved in international banking rather than domestic banks with offshore operations because such companies (like the trio just mentioned) are prohibited from conducting banking business inside the United States. Thus, what applies to them in the conduct of their international banking business may, to the degree the situation of your international bank is similar to theirs, apply to you as well.

Private Bank Risk Factors
Associated with Mutual Funds

In chapter 3, I discussed the opportunities generated by establishing an association between your private international bank and a mutual fund or money market fund. While the potential of such an association is great, there are also special risks involved. For example, if you want to be an agent of a fund, you risk not finding a fund willing to take you on. This seems unlikely, given that the fund risks nothing and might make a great deal of money off your efforts. Still, it is possible. Also you might not get a strong response to your ad or mailing campaign, making the entire enterprise impractical.

The risks of starting a fund are even greater. Start-up costs must be recouped. Investors might claim that there was mismanagement of assets, resulting in sticky litigation. Those considering starting their own money market fund should be well-versed in asset management and have expert legal counsel from the moment planning begins. In fact, expert advice should always be sought when entering a new business. Since such risks are possible, it makes more sense to purchase cash management services at wholesale and sell them to your private international bank customers at retail.

If you plan to use a fund as a way of raising capital and generating fees, you should be aware of several risk factors. Your marketing program could prove ineffective. Marketing is the most important element of success in this or, indeed, any of these programs. There are no guarantees, and poor returns on marketing may make an entire operation unacceptable.

When selling an international money market fund, you also risk poor performance on the part of the fund. Though this may be beyond your control, you may be unable to provide a competitive rate of return. Riskier still is that the returns you expected from your relatively risky cash management account are not forthcoming. This could have a negative effect on the overall profitability of your program.

Still, despite the risks involved, money market funds offer such a high profit potential and would seem to have such a strong likelihood of success that they are certainly worth investigating. Offering a range of financial services, including mutual fund and money market investments that act as economic hedges, is an important approach to ensuring the success of your private international bank, which stands to benefit in many ways.

First, capital can be attracted to the bank quickly. Second, the service produces revenues through management fees. It permits profits to be made through asset management, expands the bank's customer base, and increases its marketing exposure, creating a valuable image of stability and reliability. Finally, if the money market or mutual fund venture is successful, it increases the resale value of your bank should you ever decide to sell.

INVESTMENT RISKS

Most profits for many private international banks will not come from extending credit. They will be generated from sound investments, such as real estate and securities, made with the bank's capital. Private international banks are not bound by the burdensome investment restrictions of U.S. banking laws, giving them wide leeway to invest in a number of vehicles.

However, someone has to decide where the bank should invest. In most cases, this person is the investment adviser or shareholder. To preserve the benefits of doing business internationally, investment decision making should usually (but not always) be conducted internationally. Once the board of directors has made its investment decision, instructions are sent regarding how to deploy the bank's investment capital. From that point, the funds are disbursed and the investment made.

If there is too much legwork connected with making an investment and the lapse of time may cause the bank to lose the opportunity or prevent it from getting the best price, the bank can delegate the power of investment to an intermediary located in the United States. This can be done without subjecting the bank to U.S. taxes. The intermediary instructs the bank's custodian of funds to proceed. The bank can rely solely on confirmation of the transaction for validity. At the board's next meeting, the actions of its delegate are ratified and approved.

OPERATIONAL RISKS: YOUR BANK MUST PROFIT AS A BANK

One of the more common misconceptions of would-be international bank owners is that, once they have the bank organized and the charter in hand, all they need do to take advantage of the tax loopholes they may encounter from time to time is to call themselves an international bank, fill in forms, and wait for the tax preferences to start flowing in. The tax advantages, they reason, will be the source of their profits. Their personal wealth will increase because they are not going to be bothered by government rules. The bank will be, as it were, their private reserve.

To the extent such a scenario can be played out, it's true only in part. When an individual forms a domestic corporation, he may not do so simply to put himself in a favorable tax position. Rather, if questioned, the individual must be able to show compelling business reasons in addition to, or instead of, tax reasons that make formation of the corporation a smart move. Something of the same logic applies with respect to a private international bank. While a private international bank gets special tax favors because it's a bank and not an individual or ordinary corporation, the label alone won't protect it from being taxed to the hilt.

For a private international bank to merit tax benefits, it must function as a bank and it must do so not only on behalf of its parent shareholder but for unrelated third parties as well. At the very least, in this view, the private international bank would have to demonstrate its diligence in soliciting business from the public. It does this by being able to show it has a policy of engaging in permissible marketing activities geared to this end, by accepting deposits, by providing trust and/or insurance services to third parties, and by functioning as an investor or trustee on behalf of its customers.

Private international bank income may not come about solely as a result of its tax-haven position. Rather, it must derive from the ordinary conduct of banking business. Profit, if any, may de facto rest on the tax credits and other benefits an international bank owner claims. Nevertheless, with respect to those benefits, the private international bank (or, more exactly, its owner) will be reviewed as to whether it has been acting as a bone fide banking institution. In a broad sense, the private international bank not only may but *must* function as a special-category corporation so it can achieve for its owners the special financial and legal treatment it sought in the first place.

Now the good news. As a practical matter, given the secrecy laws in various international jurisdictions that protect the confidentiality of customers or owners, and given the record of host-country integrity in this regard, it would appear difficult for the IRS or other interested persons to break host-country law by asking who is or is not a member of a given private international bank's unrelated public. Still, the concept, as promulgated by the IRS, is worth noting as a basis for potential tax exposure. Protecting a private international bank from unwarranted scrutiny in this connection emerges as a function of sound financial management.

RISK MANAGEMENT THROUGH
SOUND BUSINESS PRACTICES

With the help of careful tax planning and the wise use of a qualified and experienced bank management company, your private international bank can both provide the public with third-party financial services and claim tax benefits. If financial transactions, services, investments, and so on must take place with the public, fiduciary responsibility is involved. Given that—and the recognition that the typical private international banker may be inexperienced in the dynamics of bank management—undercapitalization must be regarded as an intrinsic risk of private international banking.

In the final analysis, financial mismanagement cannot be blamed on government, repressive taxation, or the inability to protect privacy. It lies with the person or company controlling the bank.

International jurisdictions are "banking" on the integrity and legality of the international bank structure—not just to take in fees but to increase their status as independently governed areas as well. Lacking the natural resources of the major countries, offshore financial centers have encouraged private enterprise to bring in capital and enhance their economies. The last thing a developing island nation wants is to be seen as a financial joke.

Small reserve or paid-in capital requirements, then, are not merely a courteous gesture to attract U.S. or Brit-

In the final analysis, financial mismanagement cannot be blamed on government, repressive taxation, or the inability to protect privacy. It lies with the person or company controlling the bank.

ish capital (though this is certainly part of it). The fees are a symbol of the international jurisdiction's integrity in the global arena and its legal oversight within its own borders.

It is quite true that there are no FDIC insurance fees to pay (because, as mentioned in chapter 3, no deposit insurance is needed when a well-managed bank operates in a free investment market) and no hefty bank reserve requirements that can erode a bank's paid-in capital position before it even begins its banking business. Still, there must be adequate funding for the business of banking to take place. This is a matter of sound financial management.

Nothing in tax-haven law or custom protects a banker from an accusation of criminal liability or fraud if his private international bank cannot meet its ordinary obligations. Obviously, in order to make a loan, the bank has to have cash available to lend. And, in order to operate checking accounts, the bank must have enough capital to make sure checks drawn on it will be honored.

To diminish risks in this connection, the private international bank owner can avail himself of the various profit-making benefits of international banking already detailed in chapter 3. But to diminish risks to the assets of customers of the bank, the private international banker must also monitor developments in U.S. tax law and watch the judicial history of U.S. tax litigation.

When the bank uses money deposited for a short-term and high yield, it must, on the whole, invest that principal in shorter-term, higher-yielding vehicles. This is essential to guarantee that there will be an interest spread as profit—and that the depositor's principal, plus accrued interest, will be available for redemption if requested. Part of the private international banker's marketing function is, of course, to persuade the depositor to withdraw accrued interest only, leaving the principal (and thus the bank's working capital) on account for another period. All these activities are a function of sound business sense at its most basic, and this is why lack of financial judgment constitutes a truly major pitfall.

A private international bank's capitalization might be called seed money in any other business. A standard capital reserve, unrelated to a legal reserve requirement, is an insurance policy against bank failure. Once depositors and borrowers appear, the bank can move into the realm of statistical probability—it is highly improbable that all bank customers will want to withdraw their money from the bank at the same time.

Two things happen if a private international bank fails because of a lack of or a misuse of capital. The detrimental effect on the bank owner's reputation is obvious. More serious from the host country's point of view is that it, too, may develop an unreliable financial reputation.

The ultimate result of this situation could be a move by the host government to enact restrictive banking, tax, or reserve laws. In part, the misdirection of international bank funds in Bermuda led to that country's tougher attitude toward licensing of inexperienced international bankers whose primary purpose was the search for tax relief. Antigua, in the aftermath of the European Union Bank fiasco, could conceivably react in a similar fashion.

Turning a Risk Into a Benefit

An international bank may encounter problems for a number of different reasons. Tax laws in the United States can change at virtually any time at the whim of the IRS or a tax court. Fortunately, tax officials usually telegraph their moves far enough in advance that prudent planning before a regulation takes effect can offset its negative impact on an international bank or its owner. This is the approach taken by Merrill Lynch (discussed in chapter 5), and it can apply to virtually any offshore bank.

The greatest danger an international bank can face is the same as that faced by any bank: financial trouble. And, in virtually every case, this can be traced to ineffective management. Yet, unlike domestic banks, whose customers are protected by the FDIC in case of collapse, private international banks have considerable incentive to manage their affairs with great care.

The greatest danger an international bank can face is the same as that faced by any bank: financial trouble. And, in virtually every case, this can be traced to ineffective management. Yet, unlike domestic banks, whose customers are protected by the FDIC in case of collapse, private international banks have considerable incentive to manage their affairs with great care.

Capable management and financial flexibility not available to domestic banks can alter a risk situation and turn it into a positive benefit. Consider the following example:

Suppose, once again, that you are the owner of Commerce Bank Ltd. (CBL) and that you sold one of your depositors an international CD. The depositor has held the CD, in the amount of $25,000, in your bank for two years. The terms of the CD state that CBL will pay 12 percent simple interest per year on CDs of $20,000 and more. Thus far, your depositor's CD has accumulated $6,000 in interest. He is planning to travel throughout the Orient, and he wants to travel in style. He thus wants to redeem the CD, plus interest.

As luck would have it, another customer of yours has had a CD from the bank in the amount of $100,000. It has been in the bank for three years and, at 12 percent simple annual interest, has accumulated $36,000 in simple interest.

This investor is planning to convert some condominiums in Phoenix and wants to cash in his CD to help finance the construction. Both he and the first depositor notify CBL on the same day of their intention to cash in their respective CDs.

You are faced with having to come up with $167,000, representing the face values of the CDs, plus interest. Unfortunately, you just concluded a real estate transaction on behalf of your bank that required earnest money of $250,000. While CBL has a good deal of cash on hand and many near liquid assets, it does not have $167,000 in cash to pay out to its two customers. The $250,000 is being held in escrow at a prime bank in Los Angeles. Because of the profit potential involved in the real estate deal, you determined that it was worth the risk to deposit that much of CBL's cash on hand to an escrow account.

Your bank faces a temporary risk because two customers holding high-yielding CDs want their money at the same time and you can't withdraw the cash from escrow. If CBL can't find the cash, it faces serious liability. You relied on the law of statistical probability that customers would not want to demand cash at the same time, but in this case, a temporary cash-flow problem has arisen.

Your bank has a solid reputation in the international banking community. You are confident that you can line up a short-term loan from a commercial bank to get CBL over the hump, but you want the amount of the loan to be as low as possible. If you can, you would like to avoid paying out $167,000 in cash all at once.

Fortunately, you are not caught totally unaware. The terms of CBL's CDs specifically provide that a fifteen-day notice be given before a CD may be redeemed. From the time that you receive notice from your two depositors until the day of redemption, you have time to act in a way that will best protect CBL.

You have several courses of action. First, you can try to persuade the first depositor to redeem only the interest on his CD, not the principal amount. He need not cash in the entire principal just to take advantage of the interest. If he takes out his $6,000 in interest, he can "roll over" his CD in CBL for another term, and it can continue to accumulate 12 percent annual interest. This is a sales and negotiation job for you. If you succeed, your cash position is improved by the amount of this depositor's principal. Perhaps you can also persuade the second depositor to redeem only the interest on his CD, pointing out that it makes sense not to shoot the works in cash. Besides, in both cases, repatriating the asset will result in heavy capital gains taxes.

On the basis of your advice, the first depositor decides to redeem the interest only, figuring he can still have a nice trip to the Orient on $6,000. The second depositor, however, needs the full $136,000 now. You thus suggest that he withdraw only the $36,000 in interest owing, retaining the $100,000 CD and also taking out a $100,000 loan from the bank. This will have the effect of creating interest expense to offset tax liability he may incur by repatriating the $36,000 in interest earned by the CD. You realize that granting this second depositor a loan will also create interest income for CBL. The second depositor agrees.

Having reached a solution to his cash-flow problem, you arrange a $142,000 short-term loan for CBL from the commercial bank at bank-to-bank rates. You then pay the first depositor his $6,000 in interest, pay your second depositor his $36,000 in interest, and loan him $100,000.

You thus not only avoid having to reduce your cash position—you break virtually even on your costs since CBL receives a higher rate on the loan to the second depositor than it has to pay on its own loan from the commercial bank. And even that break-even situation will turn into a profit once CBL's $250,000 comes out of escrow and is available to pay off the short-term commercial loan. In summary, this process accomplished the following:

For the bank:

- It protected CBL's cash position in a risk situation.
- It kept principal deposits in the hands of the bank.
- It saved the bank from financial liability.
- It gave CBL a short-term break-even situation thanks to the spread between the rate on its $142,000 commercial loan and the interest it charges on the $100,000 loan to the second depositor.
- It gave the bank a guaranteed longer-term profit once the commercial loan is paid off and CBL is left to collect the remaining interest on the $100,000 loan to the second depositor.
- Most important, it preserved the status and credibility of CBL in the eyes of its customers.

For the customers:

- It satisfied their immediate needs for cash.
- It allowed them to retain capital internationally.
- It used a loan to create a tax-benefit interest expense to offset tax liability on passive income.

For you:

- It enhanced your standing as a financial adviser and negotiator.
- It turned a potential risk to the temporary cash-flow position into a positive benefit.

You would not have been able to protect the reputation of CBL had you not had excellent business management and negotiating skills. If CBL, in its turn, had not had a sound financial record in the international community, it might not have qualified for a bank-to-bank loan on the short notice that you required. Your strong management sense and knowledge of tax liabilities versus tax benefits made it possible for you to change the character of the situation entirely.

Finally, and perhaps most important from a pure business-planning position, CBL was set up to handle just this kind of contingency. Its original CD agreements specified a fifteen-day notice for redemption and withdrawal. That meant you were shrewd enough in the all-important organizational phase of CBL to provide for some lead time in raising cash quickly in the unlikely event you would have to do so.

All these factors are a function of good business practice—and sound business practices are the best protection against risk for any private international bank.

CHAPTER 9

A COMPARISON OF PRIVATE INTERNATIONAL BANKING CENTERS

O nce you have decided that you would like to establish an international bank, the obvious question becomes, Where? What's the best place to do so and why? Unless you have a compelling reason to select a particular haven, answering this question may involve the expertise of your offshore investment adviser. There are, after all, many factors to weigh.

The governments of certain international banking centers offer favorable incentives for establishing internationally licensed banks; others do not. Some centers have taxes; others do not. This chapter is intended to provide a comparative analysis of the most popular banking centers and to help you evaluate them.

There are about fifty jurisdictions around the world that, in one form or another, can be classified as tax havens or international banking centers. A number of those centers—such as St. Kitts, which sanctioned its first offshore financial centers only in 1997—are relatively new at the game. As such, they are still working the bugs out of their banking secrecy laws and licensing requirements and trying to establish a record of stability, both financial and political. The fledgling havens in this category may develop into suitable offshore banking centers in a few years, but they are not recommended at this time.

At the other extreme is Switzerland, the grand dame of tax havens, which has basically become a victim of its own popularity. For this reason, and even more because of its hand-in-glove cooperation with international tax authorities and its recently revealed complicity in the Nazi seizure of Jewish Holocaust assets, Switzerland can no longer be considered in the first rank of offshore money destinations.

And one popular Caribbean money haven, Montserrat, has dropped off the list because of an ongoing natural disaster. In July 1997, the island's Soufriere Hills volcano began erupting for the first time since Columbus's discovery of the Americas, devastating the southern two-thirds of the island and forcing the evacuation of inhabitants. Montserrat's capital, Plymouth, now stands abandoned and aflame.

In fact, on the basis of the models of success developed by experts in the field (and demonstrated by the entrepreneurial bank owners described in chapter 7), only fourteen of the fifty are currently considered suitable for domiciling or managing an international bank. These jurisdictions are as follows:

Anguilla	Grenada
Bahamas	Hong Kong
Barbados	Nauru
Belize	Netherlands Antilles
British Virgin Islands	Turks and Caicos Islands
Cayman Islands	Vanuatu
Cook Islands	Western Samoa

Before discussing each in turn, let me spend a moment on two renowned offshore centers—Bermuda and Singapore—which, while good for international banking, are currently less than hospitable when it comes to setting up a private bank.

BERMUDA

Bermuda lies approximately 600 miles off the east coast of the United States. (There are actually seven main islands, all linked by bridges.) Bermuda has a semitropical climate that is warmed by the Gulf Stream and a favorite site for big-rich vacation homes (Ted Turner and Ross Perot are shoreline neighbors). The population is 56,000 and the official language English (the island is a British crown colony).

Bermuda's favorable regulatory, legal, and fiscal frameworks have combined to make it one of the world's most successful (and oldest) offshore financial centers. It enjoys a convenient geographical location and time zone, is easy to access by air and sea, and has excellent telecommunications.

Other advantages include a highly developed infrastructure, high standard of professional and technical support services, and a relaxed regulatory environment that includes tax neutrality and freedom from foreign-exchange control for nonresident undertakings. There is, however, an agreement providing U.S. law enforcement agencies with financial information concerning civil and criminal tax cases.

Bermuda is well known as the world's captive reinsurance capital. In fact, most of the Fortune 500 companies have subsidiaries in Bermuda as part of their risk-management objectives. The island is also famous for its taxation—or lack thereof. High British taxes have no bearing on the colony. Bermuda has no tax on income, withholding, capital gains, capital transfer, or inheritance. Furthermore, there are no estate duties, no recognition of foreign judgments, and no double-taxation treaties with any other countries.

And, yes, even bankers sometimes wear shorts and knee socks!

SINGAPORE

During the banking and currency crises that swept across Asia in 1997, Singapore was an island of relative stability. Its currency slippage was held to a relatively modest 12 percent while its stock market declined 25 percent. But interest rates remained low and export growth strong, with a rebound in the region's electronics industry.

So this city-state, an independent country since 1965 and a shopping center for all of Southeast Asia, remains a leader in the financial world, attracting investors from all over the globe. Some have even predicted it could someday replace Japan as the financial center of Asia.

Many high-tech companies are located in Singapore, attracted by the excellent labor and government incentives. There is no passive income tax for resident and nonresident shareholders in Singapore corporations. Services originating and income earned outside Singapore are not taxed on profits or capital gains. Foreign income deposits do not pay withholding taxes, and dividends are not taxable. Singapore has tax treaties with many different nations, but not with the United States.

FOURTEEN OFFSHORE HAVENS

Assuming you are an investor, businessperson, or corporation of modest wealth, your goal would be to select an international banking center that has the following characteristics:

Poses little or no risk of political instability

Has the lowest annual licensing costs possible

Has the highest quality of banking regulation

Has paid-in capital requirements sufficient to both protect and preserve the integrity of the jurisdiction without unduly encumbering your working capital

Has quality facilities for communicating with the rest of the world

Is a desirable vacation spot

Has the best air connections from the United States

Has an adequate international banking infrastructure to ensure that local facilities can accommodate transactions

Imposes little or no taxation on international banking income

Maintains an excellent government attitude toward the licensing of private international banks for potential owners lacking substantial banking experience

Has an effective, well-established, and respected banking secrecy law

Here is an overview of the fourteen centers to consider in your evaluation of international banking havens.

Anguilla

Anguilla is a small British colony located at the northernmost end of the Leeward Islands in the Caribbean. Its annual licensing fee is $3,800 for banks maintaining a "physical presence" on the island (i.e., a local office and resident agent) and $7,600 for banks with no physical presence. Fees are assessed on a calendar-year basis, and advance payment of first-year fees is required.

There are no official paid-in capital requirements for private banks, but the Anguillan government does require that owners of new banks show evidence that they could meet a minimum cash-asset requirement of $47,500 for "physical presence" banks or $187,500 for banks with no physical presence, if requested to do so. There are no taxes on international banking and the government's attitude toward international banks is benign since the offshore financial industry represents the third-largest source of revenue to the Anguillan government. Strict bank secrecy laws are in place.

The infrastructure is good. Communication systems are adequate (calls can be direct dialed from the United States), the mail system is good, and the island is a pleasant (if somewhat quiet) vacation spot. An international airport with direct U.S. connections is located on the neighboring island of St. Marteen, and there are several flights a day between St. Marteen and Anguilla as well as a ferry service. If greater ease of access is important to the bank's operations, Anguilla-based banks may be managed from Vancouver or the Bahamas or through mail-forwarding services in London or Vienna.

Unfortunately, though Anguilla offers some of the most favorable features for offshore banking, at this writing the government is in a state of chaos. In fact, the island authorities are in the process of determining whether they even want to license offshore banks. Until they decide exactly what their policy is going to be, my recommendation is to hold off.

Bahamas

The Bahamas, situated in the Caribbean, is considered one of the most beautiful international banking centers in the world. It has a fully independent government, the quality of its banking regulation is excellent, and it has a comprehensive banking secrecy law. Communications systems are state-of-the-art, and there are frequent air and sea connections with the United States. There are no taxes on international banking income, and the government's attitude toward private banks owned by nonbankers is fairly good. However, the annual license fee is $25,000, and $2 million in paid-in capital is required to obtain and operate an international bank in the Bahamas.

As a result, though the Bahamas is an ideal place in which to maintain a banking presence, the high costs make it a poor choice for entrepreneurs looking to establish an individually owned private bank.

Barbados

An independent sovereign state within the British Commonwealth, Barbados is the easternmost island in the West Indies chain, situated in the Atlantic Ocean about 250 miles off the South American coast. Though 80 percent of the population is African in origin, the island's language is English. The economy depends heavily on tourism.

The government is actively working to enhance its already good reputation as an international financial center, seeking to attract new banking and financial services companies by promoting the island's natural beauty, excellent communications facilities, direct air links to three continents, highly qualified labor force (the country has a 99 percent literacy rate), and accommodative regulatory environment.

Barbados has established banking regulations comparable to those in other leading offshore centers, maintains a strict bank secrecy law, and imposes only a minimal tax on banking income. The annual licensing fee for nonresident-owned banks is just $15,000, but the paid-in capital requirement is $1 million. No institutional ownership is mandated, and no prior banking experience is required of those seeking charters. The government does, however, demand evidence that prospective owners will be engaging in legitimate banking business.

Given these factors, Barbados is currently considered the top Caribbean locale for those who can afford the high paid-in capital requirements mandated for private international bank ownership.

Belize

Belize is on the Caribbean side of Central America, bounded by Mexico and Guatemala. The population is approximately 200,000, with 60,000 living in Belize City. The official language is English, but Spanish is widely spoken.

The international airport near Belize City provides daily services to the United States and Central America. Telephone communications are excellent with international direct-dialing facilities. In addition, a satellite earth station in Belmopan, the capital city, affords high-quality telecommunication services throughout the world. International courier services for express delivery are available.

The country's position as a reputable offshore center was enhanced with recent strengthening of its financial sector's regulatory environment. New banking legislation—the Banks and Financial Institutions Act of 1995 and the Offshore Banking Act of 1996—has attracted more applications for offshore banking licenses, but correspondingly fewer licenses have been granted because of the more stringent requirements.

For unrestricted offshore banks maintaining a physical presence in the country, the annual license fee is $20,000, with a paid-up capital requirement of $25 million. Banks with no physical presence must pay an annual license fee of $15,000 and maintain paid-up capital of not less than $250,000.

If you can afford the high paid-in capital requirements mandated for private international bank ownership, Belize offers many competitive advantages, including secrecy and confidentiality provisions as well as exemptions from taxes and exchange control restrictions.

British Virgin Islands

Another British colony located in the Eastern Caribbean, the British Virgin Islands (BVI) has an annual license fee of $4,500. The quality of its banking regulations is considered poor, and there is a specific international banking secrecy law. At least $125,000 in paid-in capital is required for a banking license.

Communications systems are considered good, and the BVI are a prime vacation spot. There is one direct air connection from the United States as well as many others that involve only one stopover. The banking infrastructure and local facilities are fair. No taxes are imposed on international banking income, but some local fees are imposed. The government's attitude toward private international banks owned by nonbankers is barely tolerant.

The BVI would rate as a moderately unfavorable site for entrepreneurially owned international banks at this time, particularly since the government is not actively granting nonresident charters. However, because of the way its corporations law is structured, the BVI could be a good location for the establishment of holding companies, which can provide an additional layer of insulation between private international banks and their owners.

Cayman Islands

Like Anguilla, Bermuda, and the BVI, the Caymans are a British colony. This assures bank owners that they will receive a measure of political stability. Communications and postal systems are excellent, and the Caymans are considered a desirable vacation spot, with direct air connections from the islands to the United States.

The quality of the Cayman Islands' banking regulations is considered by experts to be the best in the world, though recently there has been some erosion of support for the banking laws because of several frauds and bad publicity resulting from being associated with insider-trading and money-laundering cases.

There has also been increasing pressure from the United States for an information-sharing agreement. In spite of this, however, the Caymans have managed to retain very stringent banking secrecy laws. The international banking infrastructure is first-rate, with ample facilities, and there are no taxes on international banking income.

A major drawback is the $25,000 annual license fee and the paid-in capital requirement of $2 million. In addition, the government's attitude toward private international banks owned by nonbankers is poor, and the government is currently refusing to grant new charters to nonbankers and nonfinancial institutions. Thus, though the Cayman Islands rate highly in comparison to most other centers, they must now be considered a poor choice for entrepreneurs and individual investors seeking a private international bank locale.

Cook Islands

The Cook Islands are situated right in the middle of paradise: in the South Pacific between Tahiti and Samoa. The population is 19,000, with approximately half living on the main island of Rarotonga. The official language is English, though Maori is widely spoken.

Rarotonga, the islands' business center, offers international postal and courier service and telephone service by satellite. Direct dialing to Rarotonga is available from most countries. Being ten hours behind GMT, Rarotonga is in the same time zone as Hawaii, which places it two hours behind Los Angeles and only five hours behind New York—convenient for European and Asian markets. International air carriers link the Cook Islands with North America and Australia.

There are no local restrictions on the movement of funds to or from the Cook Islands in any currencies except New Zealand dollars, and funds may be held and business transacted in any currency. International transactions may be conducted without restrictions in any currency or location.

The government has encouraged the development of Rarotonga as an offshore banking center. Offshore banks pay no income or corporate tax and no capital or stamp duty. In fact, the Offshore Banking Act provides that no taxation of any kind will be imposed on offshore banks, their share-holders, or depositors. And the islands are not a party to any double-taxation treaty. Confidentiality of all operations is protected by strict secrecy laws that bind government officials as well as trust company and bank employees.

For unrestricted offshore banks with a physical presence in the islands, the annual license fee is $10,000, with paid-up capital requirements of $10 million. The annual fee for more restricted offshore banking licenses vary from $2,000 to $6,000, depending on how many currencies the bank wishes to transact business in. Paid-up capital requirements are $2 million.

In light of these figures, the Cook Islands probably rank with Western Samoa and behind only Vanuatu and Nauru in the Pacific region as a desirable site for establishing a private international bank.

Grenada

Grenada is an independent country in the eastern Caribbean at the end of the Windward Island chain, ninety miles north of Venezuela. It is a British Commonwealth nation, with an elected government operating on the parliamentary system.

A volcanic island renowned for its natural beauty, Grenada has an extensive shoreline with an abundance of wonderful beaches. Thanks to considerable help from Uncle Sam, Grenada has upgraded its telephone, water, and power systems and resurfaced its 650-mile road network. An international airport, five miles from the commercial center of St. George's, offers daily flights to and from Miami and less frequently to other destinations.

Long famous as a "Spice Island" because of its nutmeg exports, Grenada is better known these days as a haven for big money. Income taxes were abolished in 1986. In its place was instituted a 20 percent value-added tax on all goods and services (except for a few basic commodities). Corporate profits are subject to a 10 percent levy on the gross sales less operating expenses. There are no foreign-exchange restrictions.

Offshore banking was established in 1996, providing for incorporating international insurance companies, offshore banks, and offshore funds. For issuance of an offshore bank license, there is a paid-in capital requirement of $1 million, but that need not be in cash, just assets. And, while the annual license fee of $20,000 is also on the high side, Grenada is probably one of the easiest Caribbean banking jurisdictions to qualify for, notwithstanding the paid-in capital requirement.

Hong Kong

Still Asia's premier financial hub, rich Hong Kong, now in Chinese control, rode out the banking and currency crisis that hit Southeast Asia in mid-1997. Thanks to its massive financial reserves, it also weathered a further speculative attack on its currency in October 1997.

Obviously the Chinese government's long-term challenge is protecting the city's status as a financial services center for Asia and bringing sky-high real estate values down in a "soft landing" rather than a crash that could devastate its banks.

In the wake of the 1997 East Asian financial turmoil, interestingly enough, some big Western conglomerates have made major acquisitions in Hong Kong. Zurich Group, the largest Swiss insurer, became the biggest shareholder of Hong Kong–based investment bank, Peregrine Investments Holdings Ltd., while State Street Global Advisors, one of America's largest fund managers, formed a joint venture with Hong Kong's Mansion House Group Ltd. to market funds to Chinese investors.

These and similar moves illustrate that the international financial community considers Hong Kong essential to Asian prosperity. But what does the near future portend for individuals contemplating the city as a domicile for a private international bank?

Under the British administration, Hong Kong was an excellent place to operate a bank, though the difficulty in qualifying for a license and the high-capital requirements put it beyond the reach of most individual entrepreneurs and even small-business or investor groups.

But probably the best advice for interested individuals today is to stay warily on the sidelines, at least for the next couple years, and watch to see what the new rulers from the mainland actually do after all the years of rhetoric. The profound hope, of course, is that they opt for a laissez faire Hong Kong policy, both economically and politically, rather than imposing repressive regulations.

Nauru

The Republic of Nauru (pronounced nah-'roo), a former Australian territory, became fully independent in 1968. There is

Probably the best advice for interested individuals today is to stay warily on the sidelines, at least for the next couple years, and watch to see what the new rulers from the mainland actually do after all the years of rhetoric. The profound hope, of course, is that they opt for a laissez faire Hong Kong policy, both economically and politically, rather than imposing repressive regulations.

little risk of political instability because of its constitutional government and the lack of an adversary political party. The annual banking license fee is just $1,500, plus a $500 local agent's fee, making it one of the lowest in the world. In fact, the banking legislation was written by an attorney who specializes in tax havens. This makes the legislation expertly suited for private international banking. The paid-up capital requirement is $100,000, having been reduced substantially from the country's early days as an offshore haven.

Nauru has fair telephone service to the rest of the world, but travel arrangements are difficult. However, if the Nauru bank is managed from another location, this problem can be avoided. It is a relatively undesirable vacation spot, but again this is not a problem if the bank is managed elsewhere since one would never have to travel there.

Nauru has no taxes on any type of income. There is minimal red tape to acquire a banking license, provided the minimum capital requirement can be satisfied. Finally, Nauru has a good international banking infrastructure and an excellent bank secrecy law, and the government welcomes banks owned by nonbankers. Given these factors, Nauru is currently considered by many experts to be one of the two best choices (the other is Vanuatu) for a nonbanker looking to establish an offshore operation in the Pacific region.

Netherlands Antilles

The Netherlands Antilles is a Dutch colony and a very desirable vacation spot, with several direct flights to the United States. The population is around 190,000, with Willemstad being the commercial center.

Offshore banking has grown dramatically during the past thirty years, and the international banking regulations are mostly favorable. However, $500,000 is required as paid-in capital, and there is a $10,000 annual license fee for an international bank established there.

Both telecommunications and international banking infrastructure are good, with enough attorneys and accounting firms to handle international business. A small tax is imposed on international banking income, however, and some of the appeal of the Antilles was diminished when its tax treaty with the United States was canceled in January 1988.

The government's attitude is also poor toward international bank ownership by nonbankers. The Netherlands Antilles does have an international banking secrecy law, but it still must be rated only fair as a potential locale for an individually owned private international bank.

Turks and Caicos Islands

The Turks and Caicos Islands are a British colony located in the eastern Caribbean at the bottom of the Bahama Islands chain. Tourism and offshore finance are the mainstays of the islands' economy, spurring local development and business opportunities. Telecommunications are adequate, and there is a supply of skilled labor.

As a vacation spot, it rates high, with direct flights available from Miami. But the quality of banking regulation is considered only so-so. No double-taxation treaties are held with any other country. Inheritance, income, sales, capital gains, gift, succession, property, and dividend taxes do not apply in the Turks and Caicos.

But, though no income tax is imposed on international banks, the government's attitude toward private international banks owned by nonbankers is not encouraging. There is, however, a limited international banking secrecy law.

The annual license fee is $10,000, and $500,000 is required as paid-in capital. In comparison to other Caribbean centers, the Turks and Caicos Islands would currently appear to be one of the less desirable choices.

Vanuatu

Vanuatu is an independent country in the South Pacific, approximately 1,400 miles off the Australian coast. The island group went through a brief period of instability in the late 1980s because of ethnic unrest and associated political strife as well as rumored government links to the Soviet Union and Libya. However, these problems have been largely resolved, and the current democratic government has issued strong public statements in support of international financial activity, seeking to reassure investors and businesspeople that earlier concerns are no longer warranted.

Financially, Vanuatu remains among the most liberal of the offshore banking havens with a paid-in capital requirement of only $150,000 and an annual license fee of just $5,000. The quality of the banking regulation, enacted in 1970, is excellent, as is the business infrastructure.

Vanuatu has an adequate international banking secrecy law, and no taxes are imposed on international banking income—indeed, Vanuatu has neither a capital gains nor an income tax. The government's attitude toward international banks owned by nonbankers is moderately favorable. Communications systems are excellent, and Vanuatu is a superb vacation spot (if you like it hot and humid). There are adequate connections for travel to and from Vanuatu.

In sum, Vanuatu is now considered by many leading offshore consultants to be one of the two best choices (comparable in quality to Nauru) as a potential Pacific base for private international banks owned by entrepreneurs or individual investors.

Western Samoa

Western Samoa comprises two large islands and seven smaller islands in the middle of the South Pacific, between Honolulu and Sydney, Australia. The climate is tropical, and the population is approximately 162,000. English is widely spoken.

Western Samoa has an excellent international telecommunications system, with international direct-dialing facilities by satellite. A modern airport provides direct access to New Zealand, Australia, Fiji, the Cook Islands, and Hawaii.

Western Samoa has a well-developed economic and commercial infrastructure. The International Companies Act of 1987 regulates offshore banking companies. The annual licensing fee is $15,800 for banks maintaining a "physical presence" on the island (i.e., a local office and resident agent), and $7,500 for banks with no physical presence. Paid-in capital requirements for private banks also vary, from $10 million for banks with a physical presence to $2 million for banks without a physical presence. Western Samoa offers a third category of offshore banking license for only $3,000 annually and requiring only $250,000 in capital reserves, but holders of this limited license "may not solicit or accept deposits from the general public."

No offshore bank licensees are permitted to advertise or solicit for banking business within Western Samoa itself. There are no obligations on minimum levels of liquid assets or debt-equity ratios. All offshore banks are protected by the secrecy provisions of the 1987 Offshore Banking Act and exempted from the imposition of any income tax or other direct or indirect tax. Western Samoa is not a party to any double-taxation agreements. In fact, no international offshore company pays taxes.

By all relevant financial criteria, Western Samoa does qualify as a suitable location for offshore banking. While clearly ranking behind both Nauru and Vanuatu in this respect (mainly because of its licensing and capital-requirement costs), Western Samoa does surpass Nauru as an island resort destination.

THE FOUR BEST

Based on the factors described, the most logical choice for U.S. investors and business owners interested in owning a private international bank would seem to come down to four offshore havens: Vanuatu and Nauru in the Pacific and Grenada and Belize in the Caribbean.

(An honorable mention, for those able to meet the steep capital requirements, goes to Barbados in the Caribbean. In the second tier of Pacific options, I place Western Samoa and the Cook Islands.)

With each of the four preferred bank locales, you get reasonably low initial and annual fees, modest capital requirements (with the exception of Barbados, which is why it's not in my top four), and an acceptable government attitude toward nonbankers. Couple these factors with a quality bank management service, and you create what most experts feel is an ideal environment for successful American ownership of a private international bank.

But just how does a person of means go about acquiring a private international bank? What are the critical steps in the process? You'll find answers to these and other related questions in the next chapter.

COMPARATIVE ANALYSIS OF LEADING INTERNATIONAL BANKING CENTERS

Country	Political Status	Annual License Fees	Quality of Banking Regulations	Cash Required for Paid-In Capital in U.S. Dollars	Communications Systems Telephone Telex Mail	Desirability as Vacation Spot	Banking Reputation	International Banking Infrastructure	Taxes on Banking Income	Institutional Ownership Required	Banking Secrecy Law	Schneider Rating
Anguilla	British Colony	$ 7,600	Fair	$ 187,500	Fair	Good	Good	Good	None	No	Yes	Fair
Bahamas	Independent	$25,000	Excellent	$2,000,000	Excellent	Excellent	Excellent	Good	None	Yes	Yes	Excellent
Barbados	Independent	$15,000	Excellent	$1,000,000	Excellent	Excellent	Excellent	Good	Minimal	Yes	Yes	Excellent
Belize	Independent	$15,000	Excellent	$ 250,000	Excellent	Excellent	Good	Good	None	No	Yes	Excellent
British Virgin Islands	British Colony	$ 4,500	Poor	$ 125,000	Good	Good	Fair	Fair	None	Yes	Yes	Poor
Cayman Islands	British Colony	$25,000	Excellent	$2,000,000	Excellent	Excellent	Excellent	Good	None	Yes	Yes	Poor
Cook Islands	Independent	$ 6,000	Fair	$2,000,000	Fair	Good	Fair	Good	None	No	Yes	Fair
Grenada	Independent	$20,000	Excellent	$1,000,000*	Excellent	Excellent	Good	Good	None	No	Yes	Excellent
Hong Kong	Chinese	$20,000	Excellent	$5,000,000	Excellent	Excellent	Excellent	Good	None	Yes	Yes	Excellent
Nauru	Independent	$ 2,000	Fair	$ 100,000*	Good	Fair	Excellent	Good	None	No	Yes	Super Excellent
Netherlands Antilles	Dutch Colony	$10,000	Excellent	$ 500,000	Good	Excellent	Good	Good	Minimal	Yes	Yes	Fair
Turks and Caicos	British Colony	$10,000	Fair	$ 500,000	Fair	Excellent	Good	Good	None	Yes	Yes	Poor
Vanuatu	Independent	$ 5,000	Excellent	$ 150,000	Excellent	Excellent	Excellent	Excellent	None	No	Yes	Super Excellent
Western Samoa	Independent	$ 7,500	Excellent	$2,000,000	Excellent	Good	Excellent	Excellent	None	No	Yes	Fair

*Under certain circumstances, this requirement may be waived or postponed.

CHAPTER 10

WHERE AND HOW TO BEGIN

You have now received a thorough introduction to the wonderful world of private international banking, the myriad ways these banks can be used, and the many benefits that can accrue to their owners (along with certain accompanying risks). You have heard the stories of corporations, professionals, individual investors, and business entrepreneurs who have turned offshore bank ownership to their advantage—in many cases, a quite substantial advantage. Finally, you have surveyed some of the leading offshore havens, with comparative rankings as to which offer the most banking advantages at the present time.

But how do you actually initiate the process of acquiring your own private international bank, and what is involved in the typical acquisition procedure? In this chapter, I'll try to give you a step-by-step review of the process.

There are vigorous debates on many issues regarding offshore banking, but on one point there is overwhelming consensus: For the actual acquisition of a private international bank, professional assistance is definitely required. This is true because of the legal and financial intricacies involved and, even more important, because of the potential ramifications of doing something wrong. Make a key mistake in the acquisition and licensing process—or even in the choice of an offshore locale—and you could find yourself exposed to the same risks you went offshore to avoid.

For this reason, there remain many technical points beyond the scope of this book that can be addressed only by professional banking advisers who have had the opportunity to carefully review your personal situation and gain an understanding of your individual goals.

The foregoing caveat, however, is intended to inform, not discourage. By no means does the bank acquisition process have to be daunting. Most professional firms operating in this arena maintain ongoing relationships with banking authorities and government officials in the most desirable offshore locales and have continuing associations with qualified bank management services. *Indeed, they already have most of the basic structure in place to help potential new bank owners quickly and efficiently complete their acquisitions and begin operations.*

In other words, they will have done virtually all the preliminary legwork for you, turning the acquisition process into a convenient turnkey transaction—modified only to reflect the specific details of your individual situation. Charters will have already been granted, necessary licenses issued, resident-agent agreements negotiated, and all banking forms and documents printed. Preliminary arrangements with international bank management firms will have been made, subject to confirmation of your choice of a desired location for the management service from among those available.

All you will really have to do is detail your banking objectives and preferences regarding bank and management service location, then wait while a background check is made to confirm your acceptability to the licensing authorities in the haven of your choice. Once you are approved, the bank charter and license will be transferred to your name, and, on payment of licensing fees and commissions, you may immediately begin using your bank to achieve profit, privacy, and tax protection. The entire process can typically be completed in just six to eight weeks.

BENEFITS OF A PROFESSIONAL BANK MANAGEMENT SERVICE

As noted at the end of the previous chapter, most American investors and entrepreneurs will be served best by choosing one of two options: one suited for those seeking the convenience of the Caribbean offshore financial community and one offering prime access to the fast-growing Pacific Rim region.

The Caribbean option would feature a private international bank chartered and licensed most likely on Grenada or Belize (with Barbados a consideration for those unfazed by its $1 million paid-in capital requirement). The Pacific Basin alternatives would be Nauru and Vanuatu, with Western Samoa and the Cook Islands secondary possibilities.

By combining the sophisticated capabilities of an experienced international bank management firm with the liberal banking privileges of a reputable jurisdiction such as Belize, Grenada, Nauru, or Vanuatu, investors can enjoy a wide range of profit-making and tax-saving benefits available nowhere else in the world. The combinations also provide the ideal solution for U.S. businesspeople and entrepreneurs seeking to increase their profits with maximum tax protection and a minimum of red tape or regulatory interference.

But the role of the international management service should not be underestimated. Few things can have a greater impact on the degree of success enjoyed by a private international bank than good management. Since most new private bankers have neither banking nor international financial experience, they must rely on the management company to perform the key administrative banking functions for them and to provide invaluable advice on how to make the highest possible profit and reap the most benefits.

For example, for a surprisingly low annual fee, a top-notch management firm will handle all your mail, telephone, and computer communications; process deposits; and keep track of receipts. It will maintain your bank office, provide typing and photocopying service, and keep up your bank's files. It will draft key documents or deposit agreements, send out bills and statements, handle funds transfers to and from the United States, and act as custodian of your confidential records, documents, minutes, books, and ledgers—ensuring the privacy of your business dealings.

Even more important, a good management company can give you foreign-exchange privileges and access to wholesale capital markets, providing specific and sophisticated international investment advice whenever you need it.

Choosing the Best Management Service

Given those profound responsibilities, your selection of a quality management firm becomes a top priority. Where should you begin looking? Again, while the entire globe may spin before your imagination, various pragmatic factors will serve to narrow your search. The leading bank-management firms are concentrated in a few geographic areas: the Bahamas, Vancouver and Montreal, Hong Kong, and, by mail rerouting, London and Vienna. The choice is yours, but my preference for most Americans, based on quality of service,

convenience, and ease of transportation and communication, is Vancouver, with the Bahamas a second choice and
Hong Kong a distant third, at least until the Chinese can
demonstrate their good intentions over a period of time.

Note: Montreal is less desirable than Vancouver because of language conflicts and the potential instability associated with the Quebecois separatist movement centered
there. And London and Vienna are merely addresses of
convenience, with actual management services handled
elsewhere.

For comparative purposes, then, the following analysis
discusses the advantages of both Vancouver and the
Bahamas.

Vancouver: Gateway to the Pacific Rim

Despite the East Asian banking and currency crisis of 1997,
the Pacific region is likely to continue its economic expan-
sion. Economic forecasters have pointed out that, over the
next ten years, 50 percent of the world's personal wealth will
be created in Asia. Thus, opportunities abound for profitable
investments. Indeed, Pacific financial centers and tax havens
are still favored over those in Switzerland, the Caymans, and
other, more established offshore financial-center locales.

Vancouver, British Columbia, beneath the backdrop of a
spectacular mountain vista and overlooking one of the
world's most beautiful waterways, is Canada's third-largest
city and one of North America's most important gateways
to the exploding business and investment opportunities of
the Far East.

With a population of 1.5 million, Vancouver also plays a
major role in international business, with one of the leading
ports for North American trade with Japan, Korea, and other
points west. It has a thriving commercial and financial center (including a sizable contingent of movie and television

> **F**or all these reasons, Vancouver has become a magnet for businesspeople and investors looking to expand their horizons beyond the shores of North America.

production people who have fled high costs in the United States). It is home to countless banks and other financial institutions and plays host to agents or offices of most of North America's major import-export companies. The stocks of thousands of companies engaged in developing the world's natural resources are traded by investors around the world in the Vancouver Stock Exchange.

For all these reasons, Vancouver has become a magnet for businesspeople and investors looking to expand their horizons beyond the shores of North America.

Vancouver offers other conveniences for Americans. English is the official language, making communication with a Vancouver management firm as natural as communication with companies and professionals here in the United States. It also has direct air connections from virtually all major U.S. cities and is easily reached by train, car, and boat from the West Coast. Cultural and business attitudes are almost identical to those in the United States, so there is no risk of culture shock.

Most important, the government of Canada welcomes investment and financial participation by foreigners, offering tax incentives and reduced legal restrictions for those choosing to base their international business and investment activities in Vancouver. The quality of service available through Vancouver management services is also quite high, and the level of professionalism is equal to that in any of the other leading offshore financial centers.

The Bahamas: Capital of the Offshore Financial World

The Bahamas enjoy a reputation as the most prestigious and desirable of all the world's offshore international financial centers. When major U.S. or international corporations decide to make their move into offshore banking, they invariably choose the Bahamas. When the world's wealthiest business tycoons and celebrities look for an offshore haven for their money and assets, their first choice is almost always the Bahamas. Even the world's most influential banks— esteemed financial institutions such as Lloyd's, BankAmerica, Credit Suisse, Barclays, Swiss Bank Corporation, and the Royal Bank of Canada—overwhelmingly select the Bahamas as a base for their international activities.

There are three primary reasons that this group of small islands off Florida's eastern coast is considered the world's most desirable offshore financial haven:

When the world's wealthiest business tycoons and celebrities look for an offshore haven for their money and assets, their first choice is almost always the Bahamas. Even the world's most influential banks—esteemed financial institutions such as Lloyd's, BankAmerica, Credit Suisse, Barclays, Swiss Bank Corporation, and the Royal Bank of Canada—overwhelmingly select the Bahamas as a base for their international activities.

1. The Bahamas enjoy almost unprecedented political stability. The islands have had their own fully elected legislature since 1729, with no uprisings, revolutions, or dictatorial confiscation of property or assets. In other words, holdings in the Bahamas are safe!

2. The Bahamas offer the most modern of facilities in a setting that can be described only as a tropical paradise. Communications are state-of-the-art; transportation is excellent, with frequent connections from all points on the East Coast, Europe, and South America; and there is a large professional community that is capable of handling virtually all legal, business, and investment needs. The Bahamas are also blessed with one of the world's best climates, spectacular beaches, legalized gambling, fine restaurants, and many other recreational and cultural advantages. And the language of choice and commerce is English.

3. Most important, the Bahamian government imposes no economic controls on international business and financial activities. There is no income tax, no tax on interest or dividends, no capital-gains tax, no estate or inheritance tax, no withholding tax, no sales tax, no gift tax, and no wealth tax. There are also no currency controls—and the corporate and banking secrecy laws are among the strictest in the world.

In short, a financial address in the Bahamas is the recognized springboard for access to today's most lucrative international banking, investment, and other money-making opportunities—and for access to the world's wealthiest people.

Unfortunately, most types of financial activity in the Bahamas are limited to an elite group of wealthy international businesspeople, major banks, and multinational corporations. This is because the Bahamas demands a high price for entry into its lucrative banking arena: a $2 million paid-in capital requirement for new private international banks and $25,000 or more in bank-licensing and legal fees.

In addition, the government of the Bahamas has restricted access to its high-quality bank management services to those financial institutions with an actual physical presence in the commonwealth. However, leading offshore financial experts have now developed a way you can establish a financial presence in the Bahamas, thus qualifying you to use the services of a Bahamian management service and enjoy the benefits of its prestigious address.

This method involves setting up a new corporation under the Bahamian International Business Companies (IBC) Act of 1989, which can be done at a far more reasonable cost. By using one of these Bahamian corporations, licensed to operate as a wholly owned subsidiary of, for example, your Grenada-based bank, you can now qualify to employ a professional Bahamian management firm. This enables you to conduct all types of business within the Bahamas, though you are precluded from doing business directly with Bahamian citizens and may not undertake any activities that would require the permission of the Central Bank of the Bahamas.

Still, the costs remain much higher than the Vancouver management alternative, and the location, requiring air or sea travel, is less convenient for most Americans. Thus, Vancouver remains my top choice as the base for your bank management service.

CHOOSING YOUR BANK LOCATION

Once you get beyond the issue of licensing costs, capital requirements, and regulatory specifics, the choice of a location for your bank is actually far less important than the selection of your management locale. That's because, with the management service handling all business and legal details, many private international bank owners never have the need to actually visit the offshore center where their bank is based—except, perhaps, as a vacation destination. Still, it pays to know as much as possible about the potential locations for your bank before making a choice, so let's review the key advantages (and any disadvantages) of the four recommended locations.

Belize Makes a Name for Itself

On the Caribbean side of Central America, Belize has continued to enhance its position not only as a tourist destination but as a reputable offshore center with progressive banking legislation. The Banks and Financial Institutions Act of 1995 and the Offshore Banking Act of 1996 have attracted many applications for offshore banking licenses.

Among the competitive attractions Belize offers those interested in opening a private international bank are these:

Secrecy and confidentiality provisions

Exemptions from taxes

No foreign-exchange restrictions

An annual license fee of only $15,000 ($20,000 for banks with a physical presence on the island)

The main drawback is the $15 million paid-up capital requirement for private bank ownership.

Unique Advantages of Grenada

Like Canada (home of the Vancouver bank management services) and the Bahamas, Grenada is a member of the British Commonwealth. English is the official language. Located in the eastern Caribbean at the end of the Windward Island chain, Grenada is being added to more cruise itineraries. More important, the island is making a name for itself as a money haven, offering many significant benefits for offshore banks. These include the following:

No income tax (abolished in 1986; corporate profits are subject to a 10 percent levy on the gross sales less operating expenses)

No foreign-exchange restrictions

Less stringent qualifications for obtaining an offshore banking license than other Caribbean jurisdictions (Unfortunately the annual banking license fee, $20,000, is not among the cheapest in the area.)

The relatively high paid-in capital requirement of $1 million need not be in cash but can be accumulated assets.

Nauru: Your Connection to the Far East

Nauru, a self-governing republic and an associate member of the British Commonwealth, is located in the Pacific Ocean southeast of Hong Kong and southwest of Hawaii. Nauru enjoys the highest standard of living of any of the South Pacific island groups, its official language is English, and it has a highly stable government. Most important, Nauru offers perhaps the most favorable overall private international banking benefits of any jurisdiction in the Pacific region today. These benefits include the following:

Nauru imposes no income tax, capital-gains tax, death tax, stamp duty, estate duty, or gift duty.

There is no requirement for previous banking experience on the part of the controlling owner of any captive bank.

The government's customary paid-in capital requirement is $730,000. However, on a case-by-case basis, Nauru offers a reduction to $100,000, payable over a one- or two-year period after banking operations begin. This capital can be paid into any bank or brokerage account in the world.

The annual license renewal fee is just $1,500, plus a $500 fee for the local agent.

A Nauru bank may be owned by nominees to preserve the total anonymity of the actual bank owner. Provisions for nominee shareholders can be arranged by the international management firm, with full retention of all rights and benefits by the bank owner.

Nauru has a very strict bank secrecy law, specifically prohibiting the disclosure of any information pertaining to any banking transactions, past or present. Violators face stiff fines and even jail.

The quality of Nauru's banking legislation is excellent. The Nauru Banking Act is comprehensive, but the regulations can be easily followed.

Vanuatu: On the Doorstep of Australia

Several hundred miles farther to the southeast, near Fiji and northwest of Sydney, Australia, lies the island of Vanuatu. Less isolated than Nauru, it offers a convenient base for anyone planning to access the markets or trade centers of Australia, New Zealand, Indonesia, or the Solomon Islands. The country suffered some internal strife earlier because of now resolved ethnic conflicts, and the former government was also rumored to be subject to Soviet influence. However, the new democratically elected parliamentary government has successfully addressed the former minority concerns, and the collapse of the Soviet Union has ended the issue of geopolitical alignment.

The new government is also actively seeking to encourage offshore financial business and has issued public invitations and reassurances regarding political and economic stability in an effort to attract new private international bank owners.

The island is relatively small (5,700 square miles), and the interior is covered with lush tropical forests, so most of the population of roughly 175,000 lives along the narrow coastal strips and near the capital city of Vila, which is also the island's financial center. English is one of the official languages, and the Australian dollar is one of the official currencies (along with the Vanuatu franc). The literacy rate is high (above 90 percent), as is the standard of living—thanks to tourism and substantial natural resources, including manganese.

On the financial front, Vanuatu is one of the most liberal—and least expensive—of the offshore financial havens. Among the advantages it offers are the following:

There are no income tax, capital-gains tax, death tax, stamp duty, or gift duty.

Previous banking experience on the part of the controlling owner of any captive bank is not a requirement.

The paid-in capital requirement is just $150,000, among the lowest of the leading offshore financial centers.

An annual license renewal fee is just $3,000.

Banks may be owned by nominees to ensure the total anonymity of the actual owner.

Vanuatu has a strict banking secrecy law.

The quality of Vanuatu's banking laws is excellent, but the regulations can be followed without difficulty.

The financial infrastructure is excellent, with the high literacy rate resulting in an ample supply of local business talent.

The island is an attractive vacation spot, with connections for air travel to and from Vanuatu. Ships from several cruise lines also make stops at the island. Communications facilities are also excellent.

BELIZE, GRENADA, NAURU, OR VANUATU AND INTERNATIONAL MANAGEMENT: A POWERFUL BANKING UNION

Combining ownership of a special-privilege private bank in the any of these offshore centers with astute, knowledgeable, internationally based management affords an especially powerful and prestigious private international banking union.

While leaving all administrative details to the management firm, the bank owner may open bank accounts in Zurich, London, or anywhere else; buy and sell all currencies; invest in gold with no capital-gains taxes; and trade on all international markets. Quickly and with considerable ease, the owner may execute just about any financial transaction worldwide and capitalize on overnight developments well before the London and New York stock markets open.

GETTING READY FOR BANK OWNERSHIP

As already noted, a qualified international banking adviser will go a long way toward simplifying your bank acquisition and, working in conjunction with the internationally based management firm, can speed you on the road to a highly efficient, easy-to-supervise private banking operation, often in as little as six to eight weeks. However, as explained earlier, you will have to undergo a basic background check, which will require you to supply the following types of documentation.

Police Clearance Letter

This letter can be obtained from your local police department or state attorney general's office. It should state that you have no criminal record. The fee for such a letter is around $10, and a personal visit to the police station is usually required. The letter should be addressed "To whom it may concern."

Bank Reference Letter

This letter should be requested from your bank and addressed "To whom it may concern" or, if your bank is unwilling to address a letter in such a fashion, to the "Minister of Finance" in the case of both Belize and Grenada; to the "Minister for Island Development and Industry, Republic of Nauru"; or to the "Minister of Finance, Government of Vanuatu, Vila, Vanuatu." The letter should indicate the length of your association with the bank, a short description of the bank's loan experience with you (if any), and any comments the banker may have that would attest to your good character and reputation.

Unaudited Financial Statement

This is a simple financial statement prepared either by yourself or your accountant. It must show that you have a net worth of at least $200,000, exclusive of home furnishings and automobiles.

CPA Net-Worth Verification Letter

This letter is a form letter that your certified public accountant must sign. It confirms that your net worth is greater than $200,000. It must be typed on the CPA's company letterhead in prescribed format.

Personal Letter of Intent

This letter is your written assurance to the host jurisdiction where you desire to situate your bank that you have no intention of using the bank for fraudulent or potentially

criminal purposes. This letter is required by virtually all offshore banking centers, including Belize, Grenada, Nauru,
and Vanuatu.

SIMPLIFIED OPERATING PROCEDURES

Once the background check is successfully completed, the
banking charter and license will be formally transferred—
and you will be able to begin normal banking business. The
operating procedures will be simple and convenient—you
simply convey your wishes by phone, e-mail, or fax or in person to the bank management firm.

The experienced management firm will implement the
administrative procedures required to carry out your wishes,
and in turn the actual transactions will be carried out (and
recorded) by the resident agent in either Belize, Grenada,
Nauru, or Vanuatu. This arms-length method of conducting
business ensures three things:

1. It clearly establishes that the bank itself is not situated
   in Vancouver or any other location where, at considerable
   expense, it would be subject to taxes and liabilities
   under the laws of those nations, territories, or colonies
   or the laws of the United States.
2. Liaison with a recognized international management firm
   allows the bank, and you as its owner, to draw on a broad
   range of sophisticated financial services and counsel on
   international currency exchange, worldwide investment
   opportunities, the raising of capital at below U.S. prime
   overseas, and many more subjects.
3. Association with a substantial management firm in Vancouver (or one of the world's other major financial centers) considerably enhances the image of the bank and
   thus opens the door to important financial contacts
   worldwide.

THE ASSETS AND PROPERTY OF YOUR BANK

When you purchase a private international bank through any of the leading offshore financial services companies, the primary thing you are buying is the bank charter and operating license. However, you should always be sure to request and get full documentation as well as other materials (e.g., bank forms) to facilitate your banking operation. Following is a list of the specific assets and property that should be included with the purchase of any Belize, Grenada, Nauru, or Vanuatu private international bank:

Memorandum and Articles of Association

The memorandum of association consists of a document executed and signed by an incorporator who is also an initial shareholder referred to as the subscriber. The subscriber, for purposes of executing the document, is allotted one share with a par value of $1. Upon sale of the bank, the initial incorporator will transfer his stock to the bank's purchaser. The articles of association outline rules governing the internal operations and organization of the private international bank.

Certificate of Incorporation

The certificate of incorporation is given by the Registrar of Companies and states that the memorandum and articles of association have been duly filed and found to be in accordance with the laws of the host country. This document provides conclusive proof that the bank has been duly incorporated and legally formed.

Banking License

The banking license is signed by the Minister of Finance in Grenada, Belize, and Vanuatu and by the Minister for Island Development and Industry in the Republic of Nauru. (See appendix B for sample.) It states that the bank is duly licensed to conduct and engage in the business of banking.

Banking Forms

Perhaps one of the most important ingredients in the success of a private international bank is its banking forms. For this reason, most quality offshore financial services firms that engage in the establishment and sale of private banks provide forms customized for each new institution. These forms are typically colorful, attractive, and in conformity with ICC rules and regulations. Usually included will be several letters of credit and a number of serialized international CD forms. (See appendix B for sample.)

BANK POWERS

In addition to the banking license and other official documents related to the incorporation and registration of the bank, the purchaser of an internationally managed private international bank based in Belize, Grenada, Nauru, Vanuatu, or other offshore jurisdiction is also endowed with certain powers by virtue of his or her position as a licensed bank owner.

These powers—essential in the legal, orderly, and profitable conduct of international banking and investment business—include but are not limited to the following:

Statutory powers

To act as natural persons

To act as attorney-in-fact

To act as officers, agents, and employees

Power to make contracts

Power to borrow

Power to create agencies and joint ventures

Power of investment

Power to deal in goodwill

Power of donation

Power of guaranty

Power of lending

Power of deposit taking

Power of trustee

Power of advertising

Banking powers

Power to provide confidential accounts

Power to issue credit cards

Power to act as investment adviser

Power to act as consultant

Power to deal in precious metals

Power to deal in securities and commodities brokerage

Power to issue securities

Power of inventory financing

Power to deal in real estate

Power to deal in shipping

Power to create correspondent banking relationships

Power to establish banking accounts

Power to create agencies

Power of collections

Power to issue licenses

Power to hold patents

Power to make acquisitions

Power to make partnerships and joint ventures

Power to be registered in foreign countries

Ancillary powers

Execution of powers

ADDITIONAL PROVISIONS

Another important benefit that should be provided by the offshore services company that sets up and sells you your bank is a prearranged provision for the registered office, resident agent, corporate secretary, and one director in the host country as well as the professional management firm's selection of two directors in Vancouver (or elsewhere).

All individuals selected should be established in the industry and possess in-depth international banking experience, thus ensuring the kind of expert support that will help in the efficient handling of your international banking transactions.

Post-Purchase Support

Your offshore banking adviser should also offer assurances of post-purchase support, expressing a willingness to provide whatever additional assistance you might need to make your new venture a success. This support should include ready counsel and guidance in key areas as well as other services. Following are just some of the post-purchase benefits many of the leading offshore advisers provide for those who purchase private international banks through their companies in order to enhance the benefits they derive from their banking activities:

- Access to books, articles, and newsletters dealing with latest trends and developments in international banking, international tax planning, and tax havens

- Current information and recommendations on new business ideas that can have a positive influence on business growth, tax savings, and the attainment of maximum privacy

- Periodic invitations to attend seminars and conferences designed to present new ideas and demonstrations of the most profitable and cost-efficient ways to operate a private international bank

Such continuing support helps ensure that you, as a new bank owner, will be able to operate and profit from your private international bank, even if you have absolutely no prior banking or money management experience.

A WORD ABOUT EXPENSES

Obviously, the offshore services company that helps arrange the initial acquisition of your private international bank will charge a fee for its work, as will the bank management company you retain to handle your bank's day-to-day operations. These are expenses that you must plan for, over and above the cost of the first-year licensing fee (which goes to the host government), any required fees for resident agents or directors, and any paid-in capital requirement. Unfortunately, it is difficult to give a precise estimate of these charges since they vary from company to company and are subject to adjustment, depending on the location you choose for your bank and the complexity of the banking and/or investment business you hope to conduct.

Charges may range from as little as $25,000 to around $50,000, depending on where the bank is located and the effort required to obtain the license. Bank management companies can charge from about $2,500 per year to more than

$5,000, again depending on the location and the amount and type of business you expect to do.

While these numbers may seem high initially, I can assure you they are not. You are paying for all the legal expertise and diplomatic ability needed to arrange a complex business structure that will comply with the rules, regulations, and political idiosyncrasies of a foreign government as well as for any experience you may lack in the banking and financial services areas. You are also paying for speed, efficiency, and ongoing support.

In fact, even with this cost, employing an offshore investment services company is far less expensive than any other method of achieving an offshore financial presence. I have heard too many woeful tales of inexperienced (and even some experienced) individuals who tried to set up private international banks on their own. Some of these people wound up spending from $100,000 to $150,000 on legal and accounting fees as well as losing as much as a year's time in the process—time that could have otherwise been spent earning offshore banking profits.

Thus, the expense involved in dealing with qualified professionals thoroughly experienced in this field will almost certainly be well justified.

A FINAL NOTE

So weigh all your offshore options carefully, but also remember this: Your government, elected and otherwise, is busily at work trying to slam all the doors to international profit potential, especially any profit beyond the long arm of the IRS. My advice is to make your move offshore while it's still possible. I can definitely tell you this: The people who have done so—after reading my books, perhaps, or attending one of my lectures and then exploring the world of offshore investment—are all dramatically better off today than they were before we met.

If you're ready to join them or just want further information, I would like very much to hear from you and, if possible, assist you in drafting an offshore game plan suited to your preferences and priorities. Who knows, there may be an island in your future.

Jerome Schneider
Premier Corporate Services Ltd.
1190 Hornby Street, 12th Floor
Vancouver BC V6Z 2L3
Canada
Telephone: 604-682-4000
Fax: 604-682-7700
E-mail: Taxhavens@aol.com
Web site: http://www.offshorewealth.com

APPENDIX A

QUESTIONS ABOUT OWNING YOUR OWN PRIVATE INTERNATIONAL BANK TO ASK YOUR CONSULTANT

I. ACQUISITION
  A. Which off-shore banking center is best for me?
    1. Belize
    2. Bahamas
    3. Cayman Islands
    4. Cook Islands
    5. Grenada
    4. Nauru
    5. Vanuatu
    6. Western Samoa
    7. Others
  B. Can we acquire the bank with . . . ?
    1. A partner
    2. A group of investors
    3. A holding company
    4. Nominees
    5. Other people's money
  C. How do I meet the requirements for . . . ?
    1. Police clearance letter
    2. Bank reference letter

    3. Character reference letter
    4. Financial statement
    5. Paid-in capital
  D. How much will it cost to acquire . . . ?
    1. A bank from scratch
    2. A turnkey/off-the-shelf bank
    3. Management services
    4. Clients and customers for my bank
    5. Correspondent relationships
II. ORGANIZATION
  A. Who should be . . . ?
    1. Officers
    2. Shareholders
    3. Chairperson
    4. President
    5. Representatives
    6. Directors
    7. Consultants
    8. Advisers
  B. How do you set up . . . ?
    1. Bank accounts in the name of the bank
    2. Investment accounts in the name of the bank
    3. Proprietary trading accounts
  C. Do we have to file . . . ?
    1. U.S. Treasury/IRS tax and informational returns
    2. Financial statements
    3. SEC and state securities forms
    4. With the Federal Reserve
  D. Should we have . . . ?
    1. Employment agreements
    2. Powers of attorney
    3. Approved bank forms
    4. Corporate minutes
    5. Fax machine
    6. Business cards
    7. Letterhead
    8. Telephone listing

9. Building directory listing
10. Management company
11. Walk-in office

III. OPERATING

A. Who should be . . . ?

1. Signatories of bank accounts
2. Authorized to purchase or sell stocks
3. In charge of the corporate books and records
4. Accepting bank deposits
5. Issuing and renewing certificates of deposit
6. Making investments for the bank
7. Negotiating on behalf of the bank
8. Responsible for loans and collection

B. Can we . . . ?

1. Maintain an office in the United States
2. Control the money
3. Advertise
4. Set up seminars
5. Solicit money by mail
6. Purchase property in the United States and abroad
7. Act as a trustee
8. Sell insurance
9. Issue Visa and MasterCard to ourselves and our clients
10. Borrow money from the Federal Reserve
11. Enter into contracts
12. Employ agents and/or representatives
13. Transfer personal assets to the bank
14. Repatriate assets and profits from the bank

C. How do we . . . ?

1. Make money with the bank
2. Use the bank for asset protection
3. Protect the secrecy of our depositors
4. Eliminate problems with federal and state regulations
5. Provide insurance to our depositors

6. Keep up with changing laws both in the United States and in the jurisdiction in which the bank is licensed
7. Borrow from other banks at the London inter-bank offered rate (LIBOR)
8. Overcome problems associated with being a controlled foreign corporation (CFC), foreign personal holding company (FPHC), and passive foreign investment company (PFIC)

D. What kind of . . . ?
   1. Accounts can be set up
   2. Interest can be charged
   3. Service charges and setup fees can be charged
   4. Schedule of trustee fees can be charged
   5. Investments can be made

E. What if . . . ?
   1. The bank is sued
   2. The bank wants to sue
   3. The law changes
   4. One of the stockholders wants to borrow money from the bank
   5. Interest rates rise or fall
   6. I have 1,000 other questions not covered by this agenda

Appendix B

Figures and Illustrations

NAME OF ISSUING BANK - NOM DE LA BANQUE EMETTRICE

BANK OF COMMERCE LIMITED

Place and date of issue - Lieu et date d'émission

Irrevocable Documentary Credit
Crédit documentaire irrévocable

Number - Numéro

Date and place of expiry - Date et lieu de validité

Applicant - Donneur d'ordre

Beneficiary - Bénéficiaire

Advising Bank - Banque notificatrice   Ref. nr. - No. Réf.

Amount - Montant

Credit available with - Crédit utilisable chez

☐ by sight payment par paiement à vue   ☐ by acceptance par acceptation   ☐ by negotiation par négociation
☐ by deferred payment at par paiement différé à

against the documents detailed herein contre les documents précisés ci-après

and beneficiary's draft at et la traite du bénéficiaire au

on
sur

Partial shipments
Expéditions partielles
☐ allowed autorisées ☐ not allowed non autorisées

Transhipment
Transbordement
☐ allowed autorisé ☐ not allowed non autorisé

Loading on board/dispatch/taking in charge at/from
Mise à bord/expédition/prise en charge à/de

for transportation to:
à destination de:

Advice for the Advising Bank - Avis destiné à la banque notificatrice

SPECIMEN

© Copyright 1984, International Chamber of Commerce / Chambre de Commerce Internationale

Documents to be presented within
Documents à présenter dans les _____ days after the date of issuance of the transport document(s) but within the validity of the credit.
jours après la date d'émission du/des document(s) de transport mais dans la période de validité du crédit.

We have issued the documentary credit as detailed above. It is subject to the Uniform Customs and Practice for Documentary Credits (1983 Revision, International Chamber of Commerce, Paris, France, Publication No. 400). We request you to advise the credit to the beneficiary

Nous avons émis ce crédit documentaire décrit ci-dessus. Il est soumis aux Règles et Usances Uniformes relatives aux Crédits Documentaires (Révision 1983, Publication No. 400 de la Chambre de Commerce internationale, Paris, France). Nous Vous prions de notifier le crédit au bénéficiaire

☐ without adding your confirmation.
sans ajouter votre confirmation.

☐ adding your confirmation.
en ajoutant votre confirmation.

☐ and authorize you to add your confirmation.
et vous autorisons à ajouter votre confirmation.

The number and the date of the credit and the name of our bank must be quoted on all drafts required. Please acknowledge receipt.
Reimbursement - Remboursement

Le numéro et la date du crédit ainsi que le nom de notre banque devront être mentionnés dans toute traite requise. Veuillez nous accuser réception.

This document consists of
Ce document consiste en _____ signed page(s)
page(s) signée(s)

Figure 1. Sample of letter of credit

REPUBLIC OF NAURU

B.L.

BANKING LICENCE

IN EXERCISE OF THE POWERS CONFERRED BY SUB-SECTION (1) OF SECTION 5 OF THE BANKING ACT 1975, I HEREBY GRANT TO:

SPECIMEN

....

LICENCE TO CONDUCT BANKING BUSINESS ON THE CONDITIONS SPECIFIED ON THE REVERSE HEREOF.

GIVEN UNDER MY HAND AND SEAL AT NAURU, CENTRAL PACIFIC, ON THIS ....DAY OF ....19 .

....

ACTING MINISTER FOR ISLAND DEVELOPMENT AND INDUSTRY

Figure 2: Sample of a Nauru banking license

CONDITIONS OF LICENCE

1. *The validity of this Licence shall expire on   or on the date the licensee ceases to remain incorporated in the Republic of Nauru whichever is earlier, unless the licence is revoked earlier by the Minister for any reason whatsoever.*

2. *There shall be paid on the grant of this Licence a sum of A$1,000.00 and in advance on each anniversary thereof a similar sum or such more sums as may be notified to the licensee.*

3. *This Licence is subject to any variations pursuant to Section 5, sub-section (8) of the Banking Act 1975. However, no variation to these conditions shall be valid unless and until such variation is made in writing by the Minister.*

4. *The Licence shall ipso facto and without any prior notice stand cancelled, if any of the following events take place:-*

     (i) *The paid up share capital of the Bank is reduced to less than US$100,000.00 without the prior written permission of the Minister.*

     (ii) *The information furnished in the application for Banking Licence has been found to be false or misleading at any time during the subsistence of the Licence.*

     (iii) *The Bank lends or raises any money or accepts any deposits from any natural person who is habitually resident in Nauru.*

     (iv) *The Bank advertises for deposits from the public in or outside Nauru.*

     (v) *All the operations of the Bank shall always be "in-house" operations.*

     (vi) *The Bank charges rate of interest on loans which exceeds the rate set by the Central Banking Authority of the country/countries in which the loans are to be made in respect of commercial loans made by Commercial Banks established in that country/countries.*

     (vii) *The Bank fails to submit to the Registrar of Banks certified copies of its audited Balance Sheet, audited Profit & Loss Account and Auditor's Report within six months after the end of each financial year.*

     (viii) *There is a change in the ownership of the Bank or in the controlling interest of the Bank, either at the level of Board of Directors or by transfer of controlling shares, without the prior written permission of the Minister.*

     (ix) *The existing laws of the country/countries in which the Bank operates or the new laws which are promulgated in that country/those countries make it impossible for the Bank to perform its obligations under the Licence.*

     (x) *The Bank, its promoters, Directors or Executives undertake or involve themselves in any unlawful and objectionable trade or activity which tantamounts to compoundable or non-compoundable offence under the laws of Nauru or of the country/countries in which the Bank operates.*

     (xi) *The financial position of the Bank deteriorates to an extent that it is not in a position to meet its obligations to its customers, creditors and depositors on due dates.*

     (xii) *The Bank fails to pay in advance the Licence fee as laid down in Clause 2.*

5. *The persons conducting the business of the Bank shall hold themselves personally, jointly and severally liable for all the acts of omissions, irregularities and violations committed by them after such cancellation.*

* * * * * * *

Figure 3. Sample of Nauru banking license conditions

Figure 4. Sample of an international CD

INDEX

Copyright protection, 140
Corporations. *See* Offshore
    corporations; U.S.
    corporations
Costs. *See* Expenses; Fees by
    banks; Licensing fees;
    Opportunity cost
CPA net-worth verification
    letter, 237
Credit bureaus, data maintained
    by, 96
Credit cards, domestic, 3
Credit cards, offshore
    profit from, 68–69
    secured, or debit cards, 68
    Visa fees to banks, 67
Credit Suisse, 229
Crime
    financial privacy and, 91
    letter of intent, 237–238
Currency, magnetic threads in
    U.S., 95
Currency exchange
    arbitraging, 63–64
    profit from, 52–53
Customs searches, 96

D
Debit cards, 68
Debt. *See* Borrowing; Loans
Department of Education, 97, 98
Department of Housing and Urban
    Development, 98
Deposit insurance
    domestic purpose of, 73
    insurers' shortage of funds, 18
    money market funds and, 72–74
    rescue mind-set from, 17–18
Depositors
    advantages of private
        international banks, 15
    as lenders to banks, 28, 48
    as shareholders, 123
    soliciting, 30–31, 34–35, 50–51

Deposits
    cash flow principles, 51–52
    cash management services,
        53–55
    currency exchange, 52–53
    interest on, 49–50
    as investment capital, 50–51
Deregulation, free-for-all after, 3–4
Developing countries, 7
Discrimination, financial privacy
    and, 90
Diversification
    for asset protection, 145
    beyond domestic investments,
        4–5
    of flight capital, 112–113
    offshore advantages, 20
Divorce, financial privacy and, 91
Docket-Search Network, 97
Domestic banks. *See* Onshore
    banks
Domestic office requirements, 43
Doran, Louis B., case history, 153,
    157–158

E
Electronic communication. *See*
    Telecommunications
Electronic credit
    ATM services, 67–68, 69
    credit cards, 67, 68–69
Equifax Services, 96–97
Eurodollar CDs, 72. *See also*
    Certificates of deposit (CDs)
Excessive government, 90
Exchanging currency
    arbitraging, 63–64
    profit from, 52–53
Excise tax, 24–25
Expenses. *See also* Licensing fees;
    Opportunity cost
    for bank management services,
        41–42, 243–244
    for international phone calls, 41

U.S. banks. *See* Onshore banks
U.S. business office requirements, 43
U.S. corporations
asset protection by, 148
international banking concerns of, 13–15
investment privacy and, 115–116
malpractice suits and, 142
U.S. laws and regulations
against privacy, 89
Anti-Crime Act of 1986, 96
areas of exposure for offshore banks, 182–183
avoiding regulatory risks, 183–184
Bank Secrecy Act of 1970, 100–102
on captive insurance, 56–57
crippling effect of, 3, 66
excessive government, 90
Fifth Amendment violations, 102–103
Financial Privacy Act of 1978, 103, 104–105
First Amendment violations, 99–100
Fourth Amendment violations, 100–102
on investing by banks, 62
Investment Advisors Act of 1933, 99–100
liability of foreign companies and, 140–141
malpractice suits, 142
on marketing by offshore banks, 37, 48

for offshore banking, 21–22, 23
privacy encroachments, 99–105
Taxpayer's Bill of Rights, 103–104
Tax Reform Act of 1976 (TEFRA), 102
Tax Reform Act of 1986, 122
on usury, 59
U.S. stock market. *See also* Stocks and bonds
international markets compared to, 6–8
percent of world market, 7–8
United States v. Miller, 101–102, 103
Usury laws, 59

V
Vancouver, bank management services in, 227–228
Vanuatu, 218–219, 220, 221, 234–236
Venture capital loans, 59–60
Veterans Administration, 98
Volcker, Paul, 4

W
Wall Street Journal, 182
Web, the. *See* Internet
Western Samoa, 219–220, 221
Wholesale banking services, 66–70
ATM services, 67–68, 69
credit cards, 67, 68–69
investment services, 70
overview, 66–67
World trade, 7
World Wide Web. See Internet
Writing style for business, 44